Bible Study Guide for Women

Grow Your Faith with Inspiring Women of the Bible and Practical Lessons

© Copyright 2024 – All rights reserved.

The content contained within this book may not be reproduced, duplicated, or transmitted without direct written permission from the author or the publisher.

Under no circumstances will any blame or legal responsibility be held against the publisher or author for any damages, reparation, or monetary loss due to the information contained within this book, either directly or indirectly.

Legal Notice:

This book is copyright-protected. It is only for personal use. You cannot amend, distribute, sell, use, quote, or paraphrase any part of the content within this book without the consent of the author or publisher.

Disclaimer Notice:

Please note the information contained within this document is for educational and entertainment purposes only. All effort has been executed to present accurate, up-to-date, reliable, and complete information. No warranties of any kind are declared or implied. Readers acknowledge that the author is not engaging in the rendering of legal, financial, medical, or professional advice. The content within this book has been derived from various sources. Please consult a licensed professional before attempting any techniques outlined in this book.

By reading this document, the reader agrees that under no circumstances is the author responsible for any losses, direct or indirect, that are incurred as a result of the use of the information contained within this document, including, but not limited to, errors, omissions, or inaccuracies.

Welcome Aboard, Check Out This Limited-Time Free Bonus!

Ahoy, reader! Welcome to the Ahoy Publications family, and thanks for snagging a copy of this book! Since you've chosen to join us on this journey, we'd like to offer you something special.

Check out the link below for a FREE e-book filled with delightful facts about American History.

But that's not all - you'll also have access to our exclusive email list with even more free e-books and insider knowledge. Well, what are ye waiting for? Click the link below to join and set sail toward exciting adventures in American History.

Access your bonus here

https://ahoypublications.com/

Or, Scan the QR code!

Table of Contents

INTRODUCTION 1
CHAPTER 1: HOW TO PREPARE FOR BIBLE STUDY 3
CHAPTER 2: THE WOMEN OF GENESIS 15
CHAPTER 3: COURAGEOUS LEADERS IN EXODUS 26
CHAPTER 4: RUTH AND ESTHER: LESSONS IN LOVE AND COMPASSION 36
CHAPTER 5: SPIRITUAL LESSONS FROM THE PSALMS 47
CHAPTER 6: GETTING CLOSER TO GOD THROUGH THE GOSPELS 59
CHAPTER 7: WOMEN OF THE GOSPEL: THE STORIES OF MARY AND MARY MAGDALENE 73
CHAPTER 8: DISCOVERING YOUR GOD-GIVEN PURPOSE 81
CHAPTER 9: DEVELOPING A CONSISTENT PRAYER LIFE 92
CONCLUSION 98
CHECK OUT ANOTHER BOOK IN THE SERIES 101
WELCOME ABOARD, CHECK OUT THIS LIMITED-TIME FREE BONUS! 102
REFERENCES 103
IMAGE SOURCES 105

Introduction

Are you seeking a way to deepen your faith and spiritual understanding of God's Word, especially as a woman? The Bible Study Guide for Women is here to help. This book is written with you in mind. It focuses on the parts most relevant to women through Bible verses and prayers speaking directly to a woman's heart. If you want a book to help you connect deeply with the Bible, look no further.

This guide is the empowerment you need to become a better version of yourself, from teaching you how to study the Bible to helping you discover your God-given purpose. It gives you easy-to-follow techniques on how to approach the Bible – and gives tips on how to prepare before you start reading. These techniques help you feel more confident and ready to understand what you read.

Women have been important to God's work from the beginning of time to today. The Bible is full of stories about strong, faithful women who played essential roles in God's plan, and their stories inspire you to live out your faith with the same strength and trust in God. This guide features several godly women and looks closer at their lives through a character-study technique. You can learn from their experiences and find inspiration in their faith and courage.

The Bible Study Guide for Women makes the Bible easier to understand by breaking it into smaller sections. Sometimes, when studying the Bible, knowing where to start or how to find the parts that matter most to you can be overwhelming. This guide solves this problem by dividing the Bible into sections, including easy-to-follow lessons. Each section is carefully chosen and written in a way you can resonate with.

This guide offers journaling prompts for personal reflection at the end of each chapter. Writing down your thoughts helps you process what you've read and makes remembering and acting on the lessons easier. These prompts encourage you to think about what you learned and how it applies to your life. They let you talk to God through writing.

If you're ready to start a new chapter in your spiritual journey, the Bible Study Guide for Women is the perfect companion to help you. Start reading today and discover how this guide can transform your understanding of the Bible and help you grow in your faith.

Chapter 1: How to Prepare for Bible Study

The Bible is a collection of God's written word for believers to gain deeper knowledge and understanding of God. It's not only one book. It is a collection of many books written by several people over centuries and generations.

You can compare the Bible to an ancient library. Picture yourself walking into a gigantic library full of old books with immense wisdom. On the shelves, you find books telling different stories: stories about the history of a group of people. Some are about laws. Some are poetry or wise sayings, and others are the biographies of influential people in the history of Christianity. This is the Bible - a library of books centuries apart written by several people with a definite style and purpose under the Holy Spirit's inspiration.

You can compare the Bible to an ancient library.[1]

Every believer is a scholar in the school of the spirit. Like how you must read textbooks, journals, and other relevant material to maintain your studies or career choice – it is the same with reading the Bible and the school of the spirit. The Bible is a book you cannot just read without studying, especially as a woman.

This first chapter focuses on equipping you with practical and spiritual tools to effectively prepare for Bible study, emphasizing the importance of creating a conducive environment, setting intentions, and introducing Bible study methods to help you make the most of your study session.

What Is Bible Study?

Bible study is like pausing from the rush of life to sit down with your pen, notepad, and Bible and learn from the deep things of God through the help of the Holy Spirit. The ultimate goal of studying the Bible is not to say you have read the bible cover to cover. Instead, it is to know God more profoundly.

As a woman, there's something special about opening the Bible, reading, thinking, and understanding what it says. Life can get extremely busy, with many things pulling women in different directions—work, family, etc. However, sitting down with the Bible is akin to taking a moment to breathe, listen, and learn what can potentially shape how you see the world and react to life's issues.

When you start a Bible study, it's like sitting down with a wise friend with many stories to tell and advice to give. This wise friend is none other than the Bible. When you commit to studying the Bible, you are guided by faith and wisdom passed down for thousands of years.

Do you remember Peter, Jesus' disciple? Remember how when he became afraid of the sea, he began to drown. Fear can drown destinies. It is usually the fear of failure that causes most people to fail. The cure of fear is faith. One of the easiest ways to build your faith is by studying the word of God. The Bible says in Romans 10:16-17, "But not all the Israelites accepted the good news. For Isaiah says, "Lord, who has believed our message? Consequently, faith comes from hearing the message, which is heard through the word about Christ."

Bible Study is not a one-time thing. It is the main source of spiritual growth for the believer. You cannot ignore the word of God and sustain relevance over a long period. The word keeps you updated with God's mind for his people daily. Remember, God speaks to His people expressly through His word.

The Importance of Preparation for Bible Study

Bible study is not only about picking up the Bible when you feel guilty for not opening it for months. That's no way to study. You are only deceiving yourself if that is your motivation to read God's Word. The Bible says in Galatians 6:7-8, *"Do not be deceived: God cannot be mocked. A man reaps what he sows. Whoever sows to please their flesh, from the flesh will reap destruction; whoever sows to please the Spirit, from the Spirit will reap eternal life."*

Studying the Bible is serious business; therefore, it requires proper physical and spiritual preparation. If you haven't guessed it already, studying the Bible after spiritually preparing your heart is one way to sow to please the spirit. As the scripture above states, you are well on your way to securing eternal life for choosing this path.

When you prepare, your mind is ready to learn. You focus more, understand more, and easily remember what you read. Preparing your mind and heart before studying is vital to getting the most out of Bible study. It leads to spiritual growth, personal development, and strong community bonds.

Spiritual Growth

Spiritual growth is one of the most essential reasons to prepare for Bible study. When you take time to prepare, you open your heart and mind to God. As you study, you learn more about God and His love for you. The Bible is full of stories and teachings showing how much God cares for you. When you prepare, you can better focus on these lessons and understand them more deeply. It helps your spirit grow stronger because you fill your heart with God's truth and love. You grow spiritually with each session, making you feel closer to God and giving you peace and strength daily.

Personal Development

All that pertains to life and godliness has been made available to believers through the word of God. Diverse stories and admonishments in the Bible teach people to be kind, honest, diligent, and compassionate. Everything you need to live a good and fulfilling life is within the pages of God's Word. These lessons are too important to be approached casually. Hence, preparation is necessary. As you read and understand the Bible, you will see how these lessons apply to your life. You might notice areas where you can improve, like being more patient or forgiving. Before you know it, these small changes lead to a massive upgrade in your character, turning you into the virtuous woman described in Proverbs 31: 1-31. You become the best version of yourself, the person God wants you to be.

Community Building

Preparation before Bible study, whether alone or with a group of women with the same vision, cannot be overemphasized. The more prepared each person is, the more interactive and fulfilling the study session. Every group member will come from a place of readiness and openness to learn from each other's insight inspired by God's spirit. Growth is inevitable, personally and communally.

The Power of Specific Goals

During your preparation, remember to make specific goals. You will need it. A specific goal when studying is like picking out the blue color in the sea of navy blue, sky blue, and ocean blue colors. Although they are all in the family of blue, if your goal is to get the ocean blue, you will naturally strive to make the selection. Right? Picking a different color or a color at random will not be as fulfilling because a goal is already in place. Your specific goal in Bible study could be understanding a scripture, finding peace, or picking out a biblical principle to apply to your life.

The Bible is full of wisdom and insight. So, to make the most of your Bible study session for however long it would be, biting small chunks so you can chew and digest without issues is advisable.

Specific goals will help you study better. For example, if your goal is to understand a topic like honesty, concentrating on Bible verses and stories that make the topic easy to understand will give you a direction to follow and stay focused.

Specific goals will help you study better.²

Besides providing definite direction, goals help you track your spiritual growth. If your goal is to pray or trust God more, you can see how well you are doing over time. Goals help you stay committed and motivated. You feel closer to God and stronger in your faith as you meet your goals.

The Need for Spiritual Preparation

Bible study is no funfair. Studying the Bible without spiritual preparation is the worst way to study. It's like jumping into a swimming pool, and you come out completely dry after spending hours in it. Not even the hair on your skin is wet. That would have been a miracle in a different circumstance. However, in this context, the swimming pool is the Bible, and coming out dry is not good. It means there is no deep understanding.

This is why people still struggle with spiritual growth, even though they can read the Bible cover to cover in various translations.

What does it mean to prepare spiritually for Bible study? It invites the Spirit of God's presence to join you for the study session. As the spirit leads, you could take it up a notch by fasting before and during your study time.

In John 14:26, Jesus said, *"But the Advocate, the Holy Spirit, whom the Father will send in my name, will teach you all things and will remind you of everything I have said to you."* The Holy Spirit is the believers' access to the deep things of God, 1 Cor. 2:9-10, *"However, as it is written: "What no eye has seen, what no ear has heard, and what no human mind has conceived"— the things God has prepared for those who love him—these are the things God has revealed to us by his Spirit. The Spirit searches all things, even the deep things of God."*

It is the Spirit that alerts you to moments in a Bible story. The Bible is full of mysteries and keys to succeeding in all facets of life.

Redemption without empowerment leads to frustration. The agent of empowerment is the Holy Spirit. The channel through which the empowerment comes is the word of God. Your hunger and thirst are the price to pay for this empowerment through studying the word. Psalms 63:1. Your thirst for God's knowledge and wisdom lies beneath the letters printed on the Bible's pages, giving you access to the power backing God's Word.

So, even though you can pick up your Bible and read until you get tired or sleepy, it doesn't determine if your faith has increased. It is not the length of time spent or the number of Bible stories you read that increases your faith in God's Word. No. Don't be fooled! The light you encounter from God's word increases your faith. This light comes from the enlightenment of your spirit and the eyes of your understanding being open.

This is why Paul, praying for the Church, said in Ephesians 1:17-18:

"That the God of our Lord Jesus Christ, the Father of glory, may give to you the spirit of wisdom and revelation in the knowledge of Him, the eyes of your understanding being enlightened; that you may know what is the hope of His calling, what are the riches of the glory of His inheritance in the saints..."

Practical Preparation for Your Bible Study Session

As you prepare spiritually, you must also prepare practically. Pick a quiet place to focus on reading the Bible without interruption. It could be your bedroom, a cozy corner of your home, or a spot outside where you feel peaceful. Choosing a time when you won't be distracted is important, perhaps early in the morning before your day starts or in the evening after everything has settled down so you can concentrate better and avoid distractions.

Next, ensure you have everything before you start studying. Of course, you'll need your Bible. A notebook and a pen are also essential. The notebook is for writing down thoughts, questions, or important points that come to mind while reading. A Bible study session without these tools is like farming without a hoe and a machete. Having them close ensures you don't have to cut your concentration to look for anything.

Take your time with each verse. If you come across a word or phrase you don't understand, don't worry. You can look it up later or re-read it to see if it makes more sense. Mentally prepare yourself to read and study until you get insight.

Bible Study Techniques

You can employ simple Bible study techniques to help you truly understand the Bible and make the most of your study time. Some are:

- Inductive Bible study
- Topical Bible study
- Character study

The inductive Bible study technique involves observing Bible passages and drawing conclusions. This Bible study technique aims to answer six (6) questions.

1. Who is speaking in the Bible passage?
2. When is the event taking place?
3. Where is the event taking place?
4. What is the Bible passage about?
5. Why is the message from that scripture relevant?
6. How does the message apply in your life?

The character study technique is another great way to study the Bible. It focuses on a particular character in the Bible and how they became living testimonies of God's faithfulness. This book is mainly based on character study. You will learn about women in the Bible and their relationship with God. For effective character study, here are steps to follow:

1. Select a biblical character.
2. Search the scriptures for relevant verses about them.

3. Use tools like Bible dictionaries and anointed books to learn more about the character.
4. Determine how you can apply the lessons in your life.

The last study technique is the topical study technique. Like its name, this technique explores topics or concepts in the Bible. The topical study technique requires you to:

1. Select a topic.
2. Research the topic.
3. Select relevant Bible verses to study.
4. Ask questions and summarize your conclusions.
5. Write a journal on how you intend to apply the knowledge you gathered.

Here are tips on how to read and annotate scripture, keep notes, and use a journal:

- Start with a prayer. Before you open your Bible to study, take time to pray. Ask God to help you understand His word and teach you. This prayer can go a long way. According to John 14:26, the Holy Spirit is there to teach.

- Go slow and steady. There is no need to rush. You can pick one scripture, maybe only a few verses, and read slowly. Keep reading and re-reading until you understand what is said.

- As you read, if a part of the scripture catches your attention, use a pencil or highlighter to mark or underline the verse. It will help you remember it easily. Also, the verse becomes easy to pick out when you open your Bible.

- After you read a verse, meditate on it and make notes. There is no need to write too much, just a few words to remind you. Psalm 1:2-3 says, *"...but whose delight is in the law of the Lord, and who meditates on his law day and night. That person is like a tree planted by streams of water, which yields its fruit in season and whose leaf does not wither—whatever they do prospers."* Meditation causes the light of God's Word to shine brighter. This is why God told Joshua in Joshua 1:8 to meditate on the word day and night.

- Don't be afraid to ask questions. When you read and find parts difficult to understand, don't ignore them or make assumptions.

Write down your questions. You can ask someone more spiritually mature or pray for better understanding. The Holy Spirit is there to help. Ask, and you shall receive, including knowledge and understanding.

- Get a journal that you can use daily or weekly, depending on your study schedule. One is enough. When it's full, don't discard it. Get a new one and keep the old one for reference purposes.

Documenting your daily finds in a journal will help your progress.[3]

- After reading and writing, reflect on what you read and pray again. Say a prayer of thanksgiving and ask the Lord to help you apply the knowledge. Luke 6:47–48, *"As for everyone who comes to me and hears my words and puts them into practice, I will show you what they are like. They are like a man building a house who dug down deep and laid the foundation on rock. When a flood came, the torrent struck that house but could not shake it because it was well built."*

Bible Study Challenges for Women

Like every rewarding and fulfilling activity, Bible study also has challenges. These challenges differ for each person. Here are common Bible study challenges women face:

- **Difficulty Creating Study Schedules:** Women usually face challenges balancing Bible study with responsibilities like work, family, and household tasks. There is almost no time to spare once they complete their daily tasks. It poses a huge challenge for them. Some women postpone their study sessions to ensure they get everything else done.

- **Difficulty Maintaining Your Initial Zeal to Study the Bible:** Building a consistent and regular Bible study habit will test you in several ways, especially when life gets busy or motivation wanes.

- **Experiencing Spiritual Dryness:** There are times when studying the Bible might feel stressful. An activity that should have been fulfilling now feels like one you should have left for another time because you can't 'feel it.'

- **Distractions When It's Time to Study:** As a woman, especially one who loves God enough to fellowship with Him through His word, distractions will likely come from every angle. Distractions could be notifications, kids, family members, or intrusive thoughts, all aiming to throw you off the path of knowledge.

- **Trying to Put What You've Learned to Work:** After studying the Bible, many people are blessed with great knowledge and understanding. However, applying this knowledge becomes a problem. Proverbs 4:7 explains how wisdom is the principal. What is wisdom? Wisdom is applied knowledge. So, getting knowledge is not enough if you don't apply it. Even Jesus talks about people who receive the word but cannot do anything with it – Matthew 13:20-22.

How to Tackle These Challenges

Tackling the Challenge of Creating Time:

- **Be Intentional About Your Time:** You can set aside a specific time each day, even if it's only 10-15 minutes, for Bible study. Little doses every day will help you prepare your mind and body for longer sessions.
- **Make Studying the Bible a Daily Routine:** You don't have to wait until you are completely free. You can read a verse or a devotional while having breakfast or during a break at work.

Tackling the Challenge of Staying Consistent

- **Don't Raise the Bar Too High:** Be realistic. Start with small, manageable goals, like reading one chapter or a few verses a day. It is your study time. You're not studying for an exam or to win an award. Take your time.
- **You Know Yourself Better Than Anyone:** If staying consistent is an issue, try pairing up with a study partner or joining a group for accountability. This way, you will always be encouraged and encourage others to stay on track.

Tackling the Challenge of Spiritual Dryness

- **Try Different Bible Study Approaches:** Pick a topic and explore. If it becomes boring, switch to character study and study about one person or a group of people in the Bible. If this still doesn't do it for you, pick a random book of the Bible to study and make notes in a journal. One of these methods will get you hooked, at least for a reasonable period.
- **Ask God:** Pray for a fresh perspective and the desire to learn more about Him. This is the ultimate cure for spiritual dryness. The moment you involve the mystery of asking God for more of Him through the word, the Holy Spirit will appear to carry you deeper into the depths of God's wisdom and knowledge in His word.

Tackling the Challenge of Distractions

- **You Are Allowed to Have Some "Me Time.":** Use it. Don't feel guilty about wanting alone time where it's only you, your Bible, and the Holy Spirit. Find a place where you can focus without interruptions.

- **Set Boundaries:** Everyone who wants to communicate with you can wait a few minutes or hours. Turn off your phone! If you feel that is too extreme, silence your phone or set it to "Do Not Disturb" mode during study time. Ultimately, you are building someone they would be proud to be around. You need your study time for your well-being.

Tackling the Challenge of Applying the Knowledge

- After reading, spend a few minutes thinking about how you can apply what you've learned. Believers are admonished in James 1:22, "Do not merely listen to the word, and so deceive yourselves. Do what it says."
- Write down insights that stand out, meditate on them, and how to apply them in your daily life.

Inspiring Anecdotes from Women and How Studying the Bible Enhanced Their Lives and Relationship with God

Beth Moore | Author

"The scriptures have been a source of strength and guidance in my personal life. As a Bible teacher and author, studying the Bible has helped me navigate challenging times and brought me even closer to God."

Lysa TerKeurst | President of Proverbs 31 Ministries

"Studying the Bible changed my life completely. It has helped me find peace, purpose, and healing."

Joyce Meyer | Christian Author and Speaker

"Studying God's Word has helped me understand God's love and forgiveness. It gave me hope, improved my personal and spiritual growth, and guided me to start my ministry."

Journaling Prompt

Create your first journal entry by affirming your goals for Bible study. What do you want to learn, apply, and achieve?

Chapter 2: The Women of Genesis

The Book of Genesis is the first book of the Bible, written by the prophet Moses under the inspiration of the Spirit of God. It is one of the oldest books of the Bible with many interesting and inspiring stories, such as the story of creation, Noah and the ark, the story of Abraham, Joseph and his coat of many colors, Isaac and his well, Sodom and Gomorrah, Jacob, and his multi-colored flock, and many more.

The Book of Genesis is the first book of the Bible.'

In this chapter, you will study the lives of a few Biblical characters. It focuses on the women of Genesis – Adam's wife, Eve, in the story of creation; Abraham's wife, Sarah; Sarah's handmaid, Hagar; Isaac's wife, Rebekah; and Laban's two daughters, Leah and Rachel.

These women experienced specific challenges that tested their faith and trust in God. Each responded uniquely. This chapter explores how they handled their situations and came out victorious. You can learn many lessons from the women of Genesis. So, grab your pen and notebook.

Eve | The First Woman of Creation

Often referred to as the mother of all living, Eve was Adam's missing rib. She was created as a help-meet for Adam, as his companion, so they could carry out God's purpose for their lives. During their time in the Garden of Eden, they had everything they needed. They were at peace, and their days were filled with joy and laughter, without pain or fear, and in God's presence. They had dominion over all things created by God.

God gave the couple one command: not to eat from the tree of the knowledge of good and evil. It stood in the middle of the garden like a shiny toy, and like every forbidden thing, it had fruits more beautiful and enticing than the rest. Eve never questioned the command, trusting in God's wisdom.

Unfortunately, the serpent used his subtle and deceptive nature to take advantage of her innocence and naivety. It convinced her they would not die as God told them, but their eyes would be open, and they would become like gods (Genesis 3:5). If only she knew that the serpent's agenda was to make them lose their place in God's kingdom. Eve ate the fruit and quickly shared her newest discovery with her husband.

They indeed became gods. However, God sent them out of the garden before they would eat of the Tree of Life and become immortals, and they rebelled against God as the angel Lucifer (the serpent) had done. In His anger at their disobedience, he humbled them by allowing them to work for their food, but He never took away their godly nature. In Psalm 82:6-7 God said:

> *"I said, 'You are "gods;" you are all sons of the Most High.'*
> *But you will die like mere mortals; you will fall like every other ruler."*

Eve was an open-minded woman, an optimist, and an excellent communicator. She had faith in God and was intrigued to see and hear a serpent talk. However, Eve's curiosity got the best of her, and she took the fruit. Her life became a testimony to the consequences of disobedience and the unending grace of God.

Sarah | The Mother of Nations

Being told you would be a mother of nations yet remaining barren for over 80 years is not something many women could handle. Sarah married Abraham when he was known as Abram and lived in his father's house. Their journey together was difficult, but she had faith in God and loved her husband dearly.

When God called Abraham to leave his father's house in Ur, it surprised Sarah because she had never known life outside her family and friends. However, instead of bombarding her husband with questions, she trusted him and believed in God, who spoke to him. They packed their belongings and began their long journey to a land they had never seen before.

After many years of trying to conceive, Sarah offered her handmaid to her husband so he could at least have an heir. However, it did not end well. Hagar, her handmaid, looked down on Sarah when she bore Abraham a son. Sarah became bitter and cried out to God.

Even in her moments of doubt, Sarah never stopped believing in God. She was almost 90 years old when God kept His promise. He sent angels, and when they visited the small family, they told Abraham that Sarah would soon give birth to a son. Sarah laughed when she heard it. She thought, 'How can I carry a child at this age,' to which the angels replied, "Is anything too hard for the Lord?"

True to His word, God gave her Isaac less than a year after the angels' visit. God, in His sense of humor, asked them to name the child Isaac in Genesis 17:19:

> *"Then God said, "Yes, but your wife Sarah will bear you a son, and you will call him Isaac. I will establish my covenant with him as an everlasting covenant for his descendants after him."*

Isaac means 'laughter,' and Sarah laughed when the angels visited.

When Isaac was born, Sarah told the people the Lord had made her laugh after so many years in Genesis 21:6, "Sarah said, *"God has brought me laughter, and everyone who hears about this will laugh with me."* He is indeed faithful.

The almighty test of faith came after many years of his birth: the sacrifice of their promised child. Sarah looked at her husband and saw his unwavering faith, so she let the child go. Sarah understood that faith is not always easy, and faith is trusting God, especially when you do not understand His ways.

The Bible says in Isaiah 55:8-9:

> *"For my thoughts are not your thoughts, neither are your ways my ways," declares the Lord. "As the heavens are higher than the earth, so are my ways higher than your ways and my thoughts than your thoughts."*

In Jeremiah 29:11, believers are assured of what to expect from God and why they should stand firm in faith.

"For I know the plans I have for you," declares the Lord, "plans to prosper you and not to harm you, plans to give you hope and a future."

This is why Sarah stood firm in her faith. Hebrews 11:11 testifies of Sarah:

"And by faith, even Sarah, who was past childbearing age, was enabled to bear children because she considered him faithful who had made the promise."

As a wife, Sarah did her best to support Abraham. She cared for her household, cooked meals, and ensured their servants were well-fed and cared for. She was the queen of Abraham's kingdom. Sarah's story inspires others to trust God, no matter how impossible things seem, because nothing is too hard for the Lord.

Hagar | Mother of the Ishmaelites

Hagar was Sarah's servant and Ishmael's mother. Her story begins when she becomes a servant in the house of Abraham and Sarah. She had to learn to adapt to their ways, to serve her master and his wife faithfully.

Hagar's life was without drama until Sarah approached her with a strange proposal. Sarah asked her to lie with her husband, Abraham, so that she could bear him a child. Hagar was surprised at the request but had no choice as a servant. She became pregnant with Abraham's first child.

This new status got into her head, and she became proud. She forgot her place and was soon displaced. Sarah complained about her attitude, and Abraham told Sarah to deal with her as she pleased. When Hagar couldn't take the punishment anymore, she ran away. She encountered an angel in the wilderness who advised her to return to her mistress, Sarah (Genesis 16:6-16).

Hagar encountered an angel who advised her to return to her mistress, Sarah.[5]

The angel told her to submit to Sarah and that God would multiply her seed. He assured her that God had seen her secret tears and would help her and her son. Her encounter with God in the wilderness caused her to have faith in Him. She obeyed His voice and went back to Sarah. Hagar acknowledged that God sees all. She called Him "El Roi," the God who sees me.

Not long after she returned to her mistress, she bore Abraham a son and called him Ishmael as the Lord commanded. Fast forward to Isaac's birth, and everything changed again. During the great feast, Abraham organized for his newborn son, Sarah caught Hagar's son mocking the child, and her anger flared.

Sarah demanded that Abraham send Hagar and her son away, but he hesitated until God asked him to listen to Sarah and assured him that He would watch over the child. After all, the child of the promise was Isaac and not Ishmael. Abraham packed food and water for Hagar and sent them away like he was told (Genesis 21:12-14).

As the duo wandered in the wilderness of Beersheba, they ran out of water, and Hagar left the boy under a tree, saying in her heart, 'I don't want to see him die.' While she wept, the boy also wept. God heard the child's cry and spoke to Hagar: Genesis 21:17-20:

> *"God heard the boy crying, and the angel of God called to Hagar from heaven and said to her, "What is the matter, Hagar? Do not be afraid; God has heard the boy crying as he lies there. Lift the boy up and take him by the hand, for I will make him into a great nation."*
>
> *Then God opened her eyes, and she saw a well of water. So, she went and filled the skin with water and gave the boy a drink. God was with the boy as he grew up. He lived in the desert and became an archer."*

Hagar raised her boy in the wilderness, trusting that God would be with them all their lives. He had promised that Ishmael would become a great nation, and she held onto that promise. She learned to trust in God and believe in His promises and was not put to shame.

Rebekah | The Mother of Israel

Abraham didn't want his son, Isaac, to marry anyone from the Canaanites where they were living because they didn't follow God's ways. So, he called his trusted servant and made him swear to go back to his homeland, to Abraham's relatives, to find a wife for Isaac.

Rebekah was an answered prayer for Isaac. The servant sent to find him a wife prayed to God to guide him and show him the right woman for his master's son by a sign. In his prayer, he told God that the right woman should be willing to give him some water and be kind enough to draw water for his camels.

While the servant was praying, God sent Rebekah his way. She did everything he asked God for with a smile on her face. The servant was shocked at how fast God answered his prayer. The servant asked to meet with her family, and Rebekah, led by the Spirit, didn't hesitate to take him to her family. She had heard stories of how God led His people and knew this was God's work.

When Abraham's servant told her family about the purpose of his visit and how God had led him to her, Rebekah didn't hesitate. Her family wanted her to stay a few more days, but when they asked her if she would go with the servant, she said, "I will go." This was a big step of faith, leaving everything she knew and trusting God's plan for her life.

Rebekah heard a call from God and did not question or delay. She immediately acted, trusting that God knew best. Rebekkah's faith was tested when she became Isaac's wife. She was barren for many years. Childlessness was seen as a curse in those days and could bring great shame to a woman. However, Rebekah continued to trust in God.

After twenty years of waiting, God answered their prayers, and she conceived twins. While pregnant, she made a prayer of inquiry about the children. God told her two nations were in her womb – the older would serve the younger. When the time came for the blessing of her sons, Jacob and Esau, Rebekah knew she had a role to play.

She remembered God's promise that the older son, Esau, would serve the younger son, Jacob. So, she took a bold step to ensure Jacob received the blessing. Some might say she was deceptive, but in her heart, she aligned with God's Word about Jacob being the chosen one. Her actions ensured God's will was fulfilled. Genesis 27:6-30

Her faith was proactive. She was willing to take risks for what she believed to be God's plan. Rebekah trusted God wholeheartedly. She was willing to step out in faith, leave her comfort zone, and make hard decisions to stay aligned with God's plan and purpose.

Leah | The First-Born Daughter

Leah was the elder daughter of Laban, Jacob's uncle. Upon reaching his mother's homeland, Jacob met Leah's younger sister, Rachel, and agreed to work for Laban for seven years to marry her. However, Laban deceived Jacob on the wedding night. He was given Leah instead of Rachel. Laban's people had a custom where the younger daughter could not be married before the elder ones. So, Jacob had a wife he did not love. When he discovered he had married Leah, he was sad Laban didn't tell him about their custom. However, Leah was now his wife, and he couldn't change that.

Laban saw his zeal to marry his second daughter, Rachel, and asked for another seven years of service from Jacob. He gladly agreed. Leah always knew that Jacob didn't love her, but instead of giving up on her marriage, she held on and trusted in God to keep her in her husband's house. She refused to be bitter. God saw her heart and that she was unloved and opened her womb.

While Rachel was still barren, Leah had given Jacob six sons and a daughter, Reuben, Simeon, Levi, Judah, Issachar, Zebulun, and Dinah (Genesis 29 and Genesis 30). After her fourth son, she prayed to God for more children. God answered her prayer (Genesis 30:17). Jacob's heart was still with Rachel, and she had not yet given him a child.

God made Leah so fruitful because He saw she had so much faith in Him. She sought His intervention in her marriage, and He blessed her with many children. Psalm 127:3 says, *"Children are a heritage from the Lord, offspring a reward from him."*

By the time Leah gave birth to her fourth child, Judah, she was no longer feeling rejected. Instead, she said, *"This time I will praise the Lord"* (Genesis 29:35). She decided to focus on God and praise Him for establishing her place in her husband's house. Leah displayed her faith in God by seeking and praising Him despite facing rejection from her husband. She continued to fulfill her role as a wife and mother.

Leah was not the preferred wife, but God honored her in many ways. Leah was the mother of six of Jacob's twelve sons (the twelve tribes of Israel), and her son, whom she named Judah (praise), was the ancestor of King David, the lineage of Jesus Christ. She found her value and purpose in Him. Her faithfulness to God led to a legacy far greater than she could have imagined.

Leah gave birth to Judah, who is Jesus' ancestor.[6]

Rachel | Jacob's Love at First Sight

Jacob served Laban for fourteen years so that he could marry Rachel. She was highly favored (Genesis 29:17). When Jacob arrived at the well where she came to draw water, he rolled away the stone from the well's mouth and helped her water her father's sheep. She enamored him. Seeing a woman tend to sheep was new to him. Jacob immediately fell in love with her – it was evident in how he spoke and looked at her.

Laban had given him a condition: Jacob must serve him for seven years in exchange for Rachel's hand in marriage. Seven long years! However, it didn't deter the young man. In what felt like a month, the seven years were over. Jacob was excited to receive the love of his life. Genesis 29:20 says:

> *"So Jacob served seven years to get Rachel, but they seemed like only a few days to him because of his love for her."*

However, when the time came for their marriage, Rachel was told to step back and allow her sister Leah to marry Jacob because of their custom. Imagine how Rachel felt, watching the man she loved marry another because of customs, unable to warn him beforehand. Rachel's heart broke, but she had to listen to her father. Neither she nor her sister, Leah, had any choice.

Jacob was relentless. He agreed to work another seven years for her, and Rachel couldn't have been happier. She felt bad for her sister, but Jacob's love was strong. She had to share him with Leah when she finally became his wife. Leah bore Jacob many sons, one after another, and Rachel became pained.

She turned to God and cried day and night, pleading with Him to open her womb, to bless her as He had blessed her sister. God remembered her. Genesis 30:22 says:

"Then God remembered Rachel; he listened to her and enabled her to conceive.

> *"She gave birth to her first son and named him Joseph, saying, "May the Lord add to me another son" (Genesis 30:24)*

And God granted her heart's desire in Genesis 35:16-17! She bore another son for Jacob and named him Benoni because he was born with hard labor, but Jacob changed his name to Benjamin.

Rachel's faith in God was evident in her waiting on Him for a child for over 20 years. She believed God would give her children, so she never stopped praying and crying to Him. Even when God blessed her with her first son, she named Joseph, which means 'God will give.' She was blessed with another before tragedy struck.

Parallels Between These Women's Struggles and Modern-Day Challenges Women Face Today.

The stories of the women of Genesis resonate with many challenges women face today. Here are parallels between these women's struggles and modern-day challenges:

Rachel and Sarah's deep longing for children mirrors the emotional and psychological challenges many women face today when dealing with infertility or delays in starting a family. Their struggle with jealousy was real. Many women today experience the pain of infertility or delays in conceiving, especially when they feel pressured by society to start a family.

Like Eve, many women today face choices that might have nasty consequences, such as career changes, relationships, and parenting decisions. The burden of these decisions can lead to guilt, regret, or loss. After making life-altering decisions, many women desire redemption, forgiveness, and a fresh start, striving to rebuild and renew their lives through growth, faith, or support systems.

Hagar became a single mother. Many women are familiar with this these days. Her story reflects the struggles of many single mothers today who face social stigma and the challenges of raising children without a partner. However, she was resilient, and as a true survivor, she raised her son to be strong and mighty in the wilderness.

Like the story of the two sisters, Rachel and Leah, many modern women get caught in a cycle of comparison and competition. Whether in careers, relationships, motherhood, or physical appearance, women today are often pressured to measure up to others. Social media doesn't help matters. Most women feel inadequate and envious of others when they see the love others get from their fans and followers. This competition is why there are not many genuine relationships between women.

Lessons to Learn from the Women of Genesis

These biblical stories offer timeless lessons that are relevant today. Here are lessons drawn from these Bible stories:

- Like Rachel and Sarah, continue to pray and trust God's timing, even when life doesn't unfold as expected. Hold onto God's promises and remain faithful, even when faced with doubt and delays.
- Learn from Eve that while mistakes have consequences, God's forgiveness and redemption are always available to those who seek it.
- Like Leah, instead of being bitter, she focused on God. He can turn you into wonder and give you a legacy that lasts for generations. Isaiah 60:22 says, *"The least of you will become a thousand, the smallest a mighty nation. I am the Lord; in its time I will do this swiftly."*
- As Hagar acknowledged, remember that God sees you in your struggles and will provide for your needs, even when you feel unseen. He is faithful.

Journaling Prompt

Create a personal faith journal entry reflecting on a time when your faith got tested. Write about how you can draw inspiration from the women of Genesis to strengthen your faith in similar situations.

Chapter 3: Courageous Leaders in Exodus

The Bible has many stories of women who displayed courage despite adversities. Some are known, while most are not. Like the silent characters in the background who get things done, these women actively serve in their capacity. Some were even more courageous than men, contributing to fulfilling God's plan for the Israelites.

The book of Exodus captures the stories of these women. They include Jochebed, Miriam, Shiphrah, Puah, and Pharaoh's daughter. This chapter explores the lives of these courageous women and how they defied the norms, took risks, and significantly impacted the course of events.

The book of Exodus captures the stories of these women.[7]

You might read about these names for the first time, but rest assured, their stories will inspire you. By the end of this chapter, you will have experienced the strength and determination of the women of Exodus. Are you ready to discover how powerful you are as a woman when you choose to be brave? Find a quiet place. It's time to study.

Jochebed | The Prophetic Womb (Exodus 2)

Her name may not be as popular as her children's, but no one would know of the prophet Moses and the priest Aaron if it wasn't for her sacrifice and courage. Jochebed was a woman of great courage and strong faith. She was a Levite and married Amram (Exodus 2:1).

They got married in the land of Egypt during the reign of a new Pharaoh, who knew nothing about Joseph and how he helped Egypt become a place of abundance. This new Pharaoh saw how the children of Israel were multiplying and sought to turn them into slaves because he was afraid of them.

His fear caused him to pass a decree that all newly born male children by Hebrew women be killed. Unfortunately, Jochebed was also a Hebrew woman and became pregnant during this period. When she gave birth and saw that the baby was a boy, she was sorely afraid.

Looking at the child, she realized he was no ordinary child. So, she did the unthinkable. She could tell God had a plan for her son's life, so she chose faith over fear. She hid the baby from Pharaoh and his minions for as long as possible. She succeeded for three months. She carefully moved him around, fed him, and protected him with wisdom, knowing the consequences of her actions if caught. God watched over her and her son.

After the third month, Jochebed realized she could no longer hide him. So, she crafted a sturdy basket, and with faith that could move mountains, she placed her baby boy inside the basket and on the river Nile. She carefully used materials that would keep the basket afloat. After praying to God to keep her child safe, she turned and walked away. Matthew 19:26:

> *"Jesus looked at them and said, "With man, this is impossible, but with God all things are possible."*

As God would have it, the baby floated to the side of the river into the brushes, where the Pharoah's daughter came to have her bath. The princess saw the floating basket and opened it. The baby cried, and she felt pity for him. As she carried the child, she was at a loss for what to do with it until a little girl ran to her and offered to help her find a nurse.

Unbeknownst to the princess, the little girl was the baby's big sister, and the nurse she found was the baby's mother. Jochebed couldn't contain her joy at being reunited with her son under the watchful eye of the princess. She finally had the chance to nurse the baby without fear of being killed by Pharaoh. She never exposed herself to the princess. She was known as the baby's nurse and had no problems with the title.

Raising the boy, Jochebed taught him the ways of the Lord. She let him know he was an Israelite, not an Egyptian, even though he was groomed and treated like an Egyptian prince. The baby grew into a fine young man in the Egyptian palace, but his heart was with his people as his mother taught him.

This baby was the prophet Moses. The same Moses God used to lead the Israelites out of slavery and bondage in the land of Egypt, where they had suffered for over 430 years. Jochebed's courage and unshakable faith in God to make a way where they seemed to be none made her the mother of influential figures in the Bible, Miriam, Moses, and Aaron, who grew up to be prophets.

Her faith and courage are why the Israelites tasted freedom after so many centuries. Jochebed is a testament to how one woman can impact generations by being brave, courageous, and having faith in God.

Miriam | The Prophetess (Exodus 2)

Jochebed's firstborn, Miriam, is another influential figure in the Bible that many don't know about. Her role in the deliverance of Israel is often overlooked. She was born during a dangerous time in Egypt when Pharaoh decreed all the Hebrew male infants be killed.

God, in his infinite wisdom, caused her to be born a girl so she could play her role without being noticed or affected by the decree passed over the land. When her baby brother, Moses, was born, their mother, Jochebed, hid him for three months. Miriam did all she could to help her mom protect Moses. She looked after him when their mom couldn't.

She was the one who warned her mom when officers or soldiers were approaching so she could quickly hide the baby. As a little girl, Miriam was efficient as the protective big sister. Like her mother, Miriam had faith that Moses would grow and become a great man. Determined to keep the child safe, Miriam would protect him with her life.

When their mother set baby Moses in a basket and placed him on the river Nile, Miriam's eyes shone with unshed tears but steeled her heart and trusted God as her mother had taught her. After her mother had left the river, Miriam remained close to the river bank, watching her baby brother like his guardian angel float on the river.

Alert and attentive, she followed the basket's movement with remarkable bravery and maturity unusual for someone her age. She watched as the princess and her maidens came to the river and hid while keeping an eye on the floating basket. To her greatest surprise, the basket floated to the princess. The princess took her brother out of the river and the basket.

Miriam boldly approached the princess and sweetly offered to help her find a Hebrew woman to nurse the baby. Pharaoh's daughter agreed without hesitation. Miriam quickly ran to tell her mother about God's miracle. The young girl reappeared at the river bank with her mother and a bright smile on her face. She was so excited (Exodus 2:4-9). This act saved Moses' life and allowed Jochebed to care for her son during his early years. She used this time to instill in Moses the faith and identity of his Hebrew heritage.

By the time she reached adulthood, Miriam was a prophetess alongside her brothers Moses and Aaron, who also became a prophet and a priest. After the Israelites' dramatic escape from Egypt, when God parted the Red Sea, allowing them to cross safely, and then drowned the pursuing Egyptian army, Miriam led the women of Israel in a song of victory. She took a tambourine in her hand, and all the women followed her with tambourines and dancing. Miriam sang:

"Sing to the LORD, for he has triumphed gloriously; the horse and his rider he has thrown into the sea" (Exodus 15:20-21)

And this pleased the Lord.

As an adult, Miriam's role among the Israelites became more prominent. She is referred to as a prophetess, indicating her spiritual significance and leadership among her people (Exodus 15:20). This moment demonstrated her leadership and her deep faith in God. She played a vital role in encouraging and uplifting the people's spirits through worship and praise, celebrating God's deliverance and mighty acts.

Like every human, Miriam wasn't perfect. Once, she spoke against Moses, saying:

> "Has the LORD indeed spoken only through Moses? Has he not spoken through us also?" (Numbers 12:2)

God heard this and was displeased with their challenge to Moses' authority.

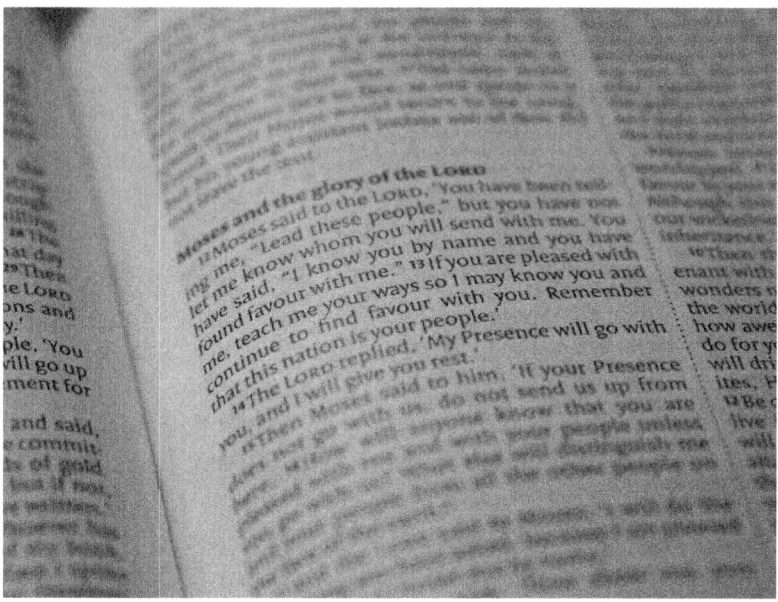

Miriam spoke against Moses, but God defended him, for he directly spoke to him.[8]

God called Moses, Aaron, and Miriam to the Tent of Meeting and descended in a pillar of cloud. God defended Moses, saying he was unlike any prophet because He spoke to Moses "face to face" (Numbers 12:8). As a punishment for her actions, Miriam was struck with leprosy, her skin becoming "white as snow" (Numbers 12:10). Moses interceded for Miriam and God instructed that she be confined outside their camp for seven days after which He would heal her. She obeyed and was healed. It was a humbling lesson for Miriam, and despite her moment of weakness, she remained a respected leader among the Israelites.

Shiphrah and Puah | The Courageous Midwives (Exodus 1)

During Pharaoh's decree to kill all male infants born by Hebrew women, God strategically placed two Hebrew midwives in Egypt to save some children. Shiphrah and Paul stood up to one of the most powerful rulers in the world out of fear of God and little respect for their lives.

Pharaoh feared the Israelites would become too powerful and join Egypt's enemies whenever war broke out. He forced the Israelites into harsh labor and oppressed them. However, instead of reducing, the number of Israelites grew. They multiplied and spread further across Egypt.

Realizing his plan failed, Pharaoh tried another strategy. He got into the business of shedding innocent blood – the blood of young infant males. He aimed to control Israel's population to ensure they never became as mighty as the Egyptians. For his plan to work, he summoned the midwives who tended to the Hebrew women because he couldn't appear the instant a child was born to kill the males.

As God would have it, the midwives in charge were Shiphrah and Puah – women who feared God. Pharaoh gave them a direct command that put the women in a dangerous and difficult position. If they obeyed Pharaoh, they would go against their conscience and God's will. However, they would face severe punishment, even death, if disobeyed. Their fear of God won the battle because, as Proverbs 29:25 says:

"Fear of man will prove to be a snare, but whoever trusts in the Lord is kept safe."

They knew that life is sacred, and God gives life and has the right to take it. So, they disobeyed Pharaoh's order. They risked their lives and freedom to let the male babies live instead of killing them. It was a brave and risky decision. They had faith and courage to stand up to powerful authority, knowing that what they did was right before God, even if dangerous.

When Pharaoh learned that the number of babies born was increasing instead of decreasing, he called the women to his palace and questioned them. The women answered him with wisdom, explaining that the wives had already delivered the babies by the time they arrived at a Hebrew house. There was nothing they could do about it. Pharaoh believed them.

God was pleased with Shiphrah and Puah for their fear of Him and their courage to do what was right. God blessed them because they feared Him and chose to preserve life. The Bible says that God dealt well with the midwives, and because they feared Him, He gave them families of their own:

> "So God was kind to the midwives and the people increased and became even more numerous. And because the midwives feared God, he gave them families of their own..." (Exodus 1:20–21)

God sees peoples' hearts and blesses those who stand for the truth, even when the odds are against them.

Pharaoh's Daughter | Moses's Foster Mom (Exodus 2)

Did you know that Moses' biological mother did not name him? Indeed not. Even though he reunited with his mom after the Nile River drama, she never named him because he was not her son – at least to the rest of Egypt and for the sake of both their lives.

Pharaoh's daughter named Moses in Exodus 2:10:

> "When the child grew older, she took him to Pharaoh's daughter, and he became her son. She named him Moses, saying, "I drew him out of the water."

From the moment Pharaoh's daughter laid her eyes on the little crying mess that floated in a basket on the river, she felt responsible for the child.

Interestingly, she knew the boy was Hebrew. She also knew the decree her father, the Pharaoh, had passed concerning them:

> "She opened it and saw the baby. He was crying, and she felt sorry for him. "This is one of the Hebrew babies," she said." (Exodus 2:6)

However, the princess was not heartless like her father.

Pharaoh's daughter took the crying boy from the basket and consoled him. She felt much compassion for the baby. While she tended to the child, cooing and rocking him back and forth, a little girl ran up to her. Her maidens tried to stop the girl, but Pharaoh's daughter told them to let her through. The girl told the princess she knew someone who would take good care of the baby. It was painfully obvious the princess had no idea what to do with the baby as it wailed.

Pharaoh's daughter consented, and the little girl disappeared only to reappear with a middle-aged, pleasant-looking woman. The princess watched with wide eyes how the baby immediately became quiet the moment the woman took him from her arms. 'This little girl is a godsend,' she thought.

She told the woman to take the child with her and nurse him, offering to pay the woman wages for caring for the boy. The woman happily agreed. Exodus 2:9:

"Pharaoh's daughter said to her, "Take this baby and nurse him for me, and I will pay you." So, the woman took the baby and nursed him."

When the child grew, his mother (the nurse) returned him to Pharaoh's daughter. She was pleased with how much he had grown. The princess took the boy and named him Moses. From that moment onward, he became her son and was raised as a prince in Pharaoh's palace.

Rescuing a Hebrew child was risky, probably one of the riskiest things Pharaoh's daughter had ever done. But she did it, anyway. Her kindness and compassion fueled her courage to keep the boy under Pharaoh's roof. Her fear of her father and his decree were less important than her humanity. She was determined to do what was right. Pharaoh's daughter unknowingly aligned with God's purpose and made a name for herself as a great woman in the Bible.

Rescuing a Hebrew child was risky, probably one of the riskiest things Pharaoh's daughter had ever done.[9]

The story of Moses and the deliverance of Israel cannot be recounted without mentioning the kind and courageous princess. She could have easily turned a blind eye to the floating basket or had the baby presented to her father when she saw he was Hebrew. Hence, a divine Pharaoh's daughter became an influential figure in Israel's history intervention. She understood God's purpose for this child and was ready to play her part in it, even if it went against her people.

Lessons to Learn from the Courageous Women of Exodus

You can learn many lessons from Jochebed, Miriam, Shiphrah, Puah, and Pharaoh's daughter. These women acted bravely under challenging situations and wrote their names in the sands of time. They became icons, women known for their courage, faith in God, and compassion for humanity.

You can see a good display of the power of a mother's love and faith in the story of Jochebed. Despite the fear and danger that clouded the land, Jochebed chose to protect her son. She hid Moses for three months, bravely keeping him safe even though she knew she would be severely punished if caught.

She displayed more of her brave side as she set the baby on the river because she did not know what would happen to him. From Jochebed's story, you learn that courage is trusting in a plan greater than yours, even when the future is uncertain, not just jumping headfirst into a situation. Her faith in God's plan for her son gave her the strength to let him go. Would you have done the same if you were in her shoes?

The courageous big sister, Miriam, took responsibility at a young age. As she watched the basket float away from her mother on its own accord, she couldn't do much to help her brother, but she stayed. She couldn't swim to the baby if the basket suddenly got punctured and sank. She watched him go regardless.

The little girl knew something the adults didn't, and she was there for it. She wanted to ensure nothing happened to her baby brother. Miriam quickly seized the opportunity when Pharaoh's daughter found the basket and saw Moses inside. Sometimes, opportunities can be spotted from a mile away if people are as discerning as Miriam. They can make the most of it as God would have wanted. Miriam painted a clear picture in her story: courage is not about age or size; it is willing to step up and help when things don't go as smoothly as expected. It means being watchful, wise, and ready to act, even when scared or unsure.

The two Hebrew midwives feared the Pharaoh, but their fear of God was greater. Are you a person who fears God? Will you willingly go against laws if they do not align with God's will? It's usually easier said than done, but Shiphrah and Puah proved that with their courage, it was doable. They blatantly disobeyed the Pharaoh and used their wisdom to evade punishment. Their actions could have cost them everything, but they put God first.

Matthew 6:33 says:

> *"But seek first his kingdom and his righteousness, and all these things will be given to you as well."* God let those baby boys live and gave them families. John 12:25 says, *"Anyone who loves their life will lose it, while anyone who hates their life in this world will keep it for eternal life."*

These women loved not their lives. Instead, they dedicated their lives to ensuring the Hebrew children were born and grew mighty no matter the cost.

What about Pharaoh's daughter? She was the daughter of the man who ordered the killings of the babies, yet she was unafraid to keep one under his roof. She took Moses into her home and raised him as her son, even though she knew it went against her father's rule.

Courage means following your heart and being kind, even when it goes against what people expect from you, like Pharaoh's daughter, so long as it is right in God's eyes. Being kind can lead to brave decisions, and compassion is strength.

Courage comes in many forms. You can see how it is beautifully displayed in these women's lives. It can be shown through faith, responsibility, doing what is right, or being compassionate.

Journaling Prompt

Write a letter to one of the women in Exodus that inspires you. Tell her about your struggles and how her story of bravery and resilience helped you.

Chapter 4: Ruth and Esther: Lessons in Love and Compassion

Love and compassion are two vital tenets of a good Christian. Indeed, a good person. Apostle Paul, speaking on love, wrote an entire chapter to remind believers of the importance of love.

Love and compassion are two vital tenets of a good Christian.[10]

1 Corinthians 13:1-13:

> *"If I speak in the tongues of men or of angels, but do not have love, I am only a resounding gong or a clanging cymbal. If I have the gift of prophecy and can fathom all mysteries and all knowledge, and if I have a faith that can move mountains, but do not have love, I am nothing. If I give all I possess to the poor and give over my body to hardship that I may boast, but do not have love, I gain nothing. Love is patient, love is kind. It does not envy, it does not boast, it is not proud. It does not dishonor others, it is not self-seeking, it is not easily angered, it keeps no record of wrongs. Love does not delight in evil but rejoices with the truth. It always protects, always trusts, always hopes, always perseveres. Love never fails. But where there are prophecies, they will cease; where there are tongues, they will be stilled; where there is knowledge, it will pass away. For we know in part, and we prophesy in part, but when completeness comes, what is in part disappears. When I was a child, I talked like a child, I thought like a child, I reasoned like a child. When I became a man, I put the ways of childhood behind me. For now, we see only a reflection as in a mirror; then we shall see face to face. Now I know in part; then I shall know fully, even as I am fully known. And now these three remain: faith, hope, and love. But the greatest of these is love."*

Now, if your love looks nothing like the love described above, you have some work to do. Lucky for you, this chapter will guide you when you are confused about what love should look like.

Jesus taught about love during His time on earth. In John 13:34, he said:

> *"A new command I give you: Love one another. As I have loved you, so you must love one another."*

Matthew 22:34-40:

> *"Hearing that Jesus had silenced the Sadducees, the Pharisees got together. One of them, an expert in the law, tested him with this question: "Teacher, which is the greatest commandment in the Law?" Jesus replied: "Love the Lord your God with all your heart and with all your soul and with all your mind. This is the first and greatest commandment.*

And the second is like it: Love your neighbor as yourself. All the Law and the Prophets hang on these two commandments."

This chapter is about love, love, and more love. Right next to the theme of love is compassion. God is a loving and compassionate father. Micah 7:18 says:

"Who is a God like you, who pardons sin and forgives the transgression of the remnant of his inheritance? You do not stay angry forever but delight to show mercy." In John 3:16, the Bible states, "For God so loved the world that he gave his one and only Son, that whoever believes in him shall not perish but have eternal life."

God is love. John the Beloved confirms this in 1 John 4:7-12:

"Dear friends, let us love one another, for love comes from God. Everyone who loves has been born of God and knows God. Whoever does not love does not know God because God is love. This is how God showed his love among us: He sent his one and only Son into the world that we might live through him. This is love: not that we loved God, but that he loved us and sent his Son as an atoning sacrifice for our sins. Dear friends, since God so loved us, we also ought to love one another. No one has ever seen God, but if we love one another, God lives in us, and his love is made complete in us."

Many characters in the Bible showcase love and compassion. This chapter focuses on two spectacular women in the Old Testament, Ruth and Esther. They had love and compassion embedded in their stories. These women displayed remarkable selflessness, compassion, loyalty, courage, and, most importantly, love.

The Story of Ruth

For a time in Israel, the people did not have a king. Instead, God raised leaders, "judges," to guide the people; this era was known as the "era of judges." The book lies between the book of Ruth and the book of Joshua.

When Joshua died, there was no one to rule or lead the people like Moses had, giving rise to the need for judges in the land. However, the people of Israel had a problem. They were fundamentally stubborn and disobedient. Sometimes, they worshipped other gods or did things entirely against God's commands.

They went against the covenant God made with Abraham so many times with their tendency to idolize manmade gods.

"I will establish my covenant as an everlasting covenant between me and you and your descendants after you for the generations to come, to be your God and the God of your descendants after you" (Genesis 17:7)

Due to their behavior, God allowed difficult situations, like famine or enemy attacks, as punishment. The people cried out to God when the suffering became too much. He showed mercy by raising another judge to save them. It was a never-ending cycle with Israel.

There was a famine during this time in the small town of Bethlehem. Yes. The same Bethlehem where Jesus was born. People were suffering from the drought and crops were dying, which meant no food for the masses. A man named Elimelek from Bethlehem took his family to Moab, a nearby country, because of the famine. He ran away from the land God gave his people because the suffering was too much.

Elimelek took his wife, Naomi, and their two sons with him. It was a difficult decision to leave since Moab and Israel were not on friendly terms, and often the tension brewed between them. However, Elimelek believed that going to a place where they could find food, even if it were an enemy land, would be better.

Unfortunately for the small family, tragedy struck. Elimelek died not long after they arrived in Moab. His sons, who took wives from the Moabites, died 10 years later, leaving Elimelek's wife, Naomi, and his sons' wives, Ruth and Orpah, widows. After burning her husband and sons, Naomi heard that God had remembered Bethlehem, and the famine was over. So, she prepared to return to her homeland.

Naomi called her daughters-in-law and advised them to go to their mother's houses and find new husbands since they were still young. It was an emotional day for the women. They wept bitterly. The young women told their mother-in-law they would willingly go with her wherever she went.

Naomi tried to convince them:

"But Naomi said, "Return home, my daughters. Why would you come with me? Am I going to have any more sons, who could become your husbands? Return home, my daughters; I am too old to have another husband. Even if I thought there was still hope for me—even if I had a husband tonight

and then gave birth to sons— would you wait until they grew up? Would you remain unmarried for them? No, my daughters. It is more bitter for me than for you, because the LORD's hand has turned against me!" (Ruth 1:11-13)

Ruth was committed to caring for her late husband's mother.[11]

Orpah saw sense in Naomi's words and returned to her mother's house. She kissed Naomi, packed up her belongings, and left. On the other hand, Ruth wasn't willing to let go of her mother-in-law. Naomi looked at her and said, *"Look, said Naomi, your sister-in-law is going back to her people and her gods. Go back with her."* But Ruth didn't budge.

She told Naomi in Ruth 1:16-17:

"Don't urge me to leave you or to turn back from you. Where you go I will go, and where you stay I will stay. Your people will be my people and your God my God. Where you die I will die, and there I will be buried. May the Lord deal with me, be it ever so severely, if even death separates you and me."

Naomi realized Ruth was determined to travel with her. She was deeply touched. She stopped urging Ruth to leave, and they returned to Bethlehem together.

Ruth was committed to caring for her late husband's mother. The woman was already old and could do very little for herself. She made a vow to follow Naomi to the ends of the earth, and she meant it.

While they were in Bethlehem, Ruth went to the fields to gather leftover grain for her and her mother-in-law. With Naomi's blessing, she set out and found herself in a field belonging to one of late Elimelek's distant relatives. The field owner, Boaz, came to greet the harvesters, and Ruth caught his eye. She wasn't a familiar face but had a beautiful face, and Boaz couldn't help but ask the overseer of his harvesters about her.

The overseer explained how Ruth came to the field and humbly asked to pick up the leftover grains as the harvesters did their job. She worked tirelessly. The overseer told him about her kindness toward her mother-in-law, whom she followed from Moab into a foreign land.

After hearing about Ruth's story, Boaz called Ruth and told her she could work in his field permanently. He commanded the men in his field not to touch her and provided everything she needed to be comfortable in his field. Ruth was surprised at his kindness toward her when he barely knew her. Boaz smiled and told her he had heard her troubles and her kindness to Naomi and assured her she would be safe with him (Ruth 2:8-11).

Boaz called her to eat with the harvesters at dinner time and offered her food. She ate until satisfied and even had some to take home to Naomi. When she left the field, Boaz ensured Ruth had more than enough grain to take home for her and Naomi.

Ruth 2:15-18:

> *"As she got up to glean, Boaz gave orders to his men, "Let her gather among the sheaves and don't reprimand her. Even pull out some stalks for her from the bundles and leave them for her to pick up, and don't rebuke her." So, Ruth gleaned in the field until evening. Then she threshed the barley she had gathered, and it amounted to about an ephah. She carried it back to town, and her mother-in-law saw how much she had gathered. Ruth also brought out and gave her what she had left over after she had eaten enough."*

Back home, Naomi couldn't believe her eyes when she saw Ruth. The younger woman told her all that transpired between her and Boaz at the field. Naomi advised her to continue working in his field because he was obviously fond of her.

After learning that Boaz was a relative who could redeem their property, Naomi devised a plan. Following Naomi's guidance, Ruth approached Boaz on the threshing floor, humbly asking him to spread his cloak over her as a symbol of protection and redemption. Boaz, moved by her request, agreed, but there was a closer relative who had the first right to redeem. Not wanting to miss his chance, Boaz quickly went to the town gate the next day to present his case- Boaz was freed to act as the kinsman-redeemer for Naomi and Ruth.

Boaz declared his intention to redeem Naomi's land and marry Ruth. The elders and people blessed the union, saying:

> *"May the Lord make the woman who is coming into your home like Rachel and Leah, who together built up the house of Israel"* (Ruth 4:11).

Boaz and Ruth married, and God blessed them with a son, Obed. Once filled with bitterness and despair, Naomi held her grandson in her arms – her joy and hope restored. The town's women celebrated with her, saying:

> *"Praise be to the Lord, who this day has not left you without a guardian-redeemer. May he become famous throughout Israel! He will renew your life and sustain you in your old age. For your daughter-in-law, who loves you and who is better to you than seven sons, has given him birth."* (Ruth 4:14-15)

Obed would become the grandfather of King David, linking Ruth, a Moabite woman, into the lineage of Israel's greatest King and Savior of the world, Jesus Christ.

The Story of Queen Esther

At one time in history, Jewish people lived under Persian rule, exiled from their homeland. King Xerxes, who knew nothing about the Jewish people, ruled the Persian Empire. The Israelites weren't numerous and surrounded by people who didn't understand or respect their faith.

Although they lived and worked in the empire, they always risked persecution. A high-ranking official in King Xerxes' court, Haman, developed a hatred for the Jewish people, causing them to live in fear.

Haman's hatred was personal. He encountered Mordecai at the gate, a Jew who refused to bow to him. In his anger, Haman plotted to destroy all the Jews in the empire, convincing King Xerxes to issue a decree to have them killed (Esther 3:8-11).

While the feud between Haman and Mordecai lurked. A different drama was unfolding in the palace. King Xerxes dismissed his wife, Queen Vashti, because of her attitude, creating a vacuum in the palace and a need for a new queen. The King's servants suggested he permit them to search the kingdom for young virgins to select a new queen. The King gave his word, and the search began.

Mordecai was the orphaned Jewish girl Esther's uncle. As soon as he heard of the King's request, he recruited Esther. She was very beautiful, and Mordecai had no doubt she would be selected.

When presented to the King, Esther found favor in his sight, and he selected her to be his new queen.[12]

When Esther made it to the palace for selection, she found favor with Hegai, the keeper of the women. He gave her special oils and quickly gave her what she needed to win the King's heart. When presented to the King, Esther found favor in his sight, and he selected her to be his new queen. Esther's status was changed overnight – from the orphaned Jewish girl to the new queen of the Persian Empire. (Esther 2:7-17). Esther's rise to queen was part of a divine plan. Mordecai, who had cared for Esther, instructed her not to reveal her Jewish identity (Esther 2:10).

Once, Mordecai overheard people discussing the assassination of the King and told Esther. She quickly informed the King. He immediately investigated and learned that, indeed, plans to assassinate him were afoot. King Xerxes had the suspects hanged, and Mordecai's name was written in the King's book of Chronicles (Esther 2:21-23).

Esther had become queen, so Mordecai discussed the problem of the Jews with her, particularly Haman's role. When Mordecai learned of Haman's plan to destroy the Jews, he tore his clothes and put on sackcloth and ashes, mourning for his people (Esther 4:1).

He sent word to Esther, urging her to go to the king and beg for mercy on behalf of her people. It seemed a simple request. However, in Persian law, anyone who approached the king without being summoned could be put to death unless the king extended his golden scepter to them (Esther 4:11).

Esther was determined to deliver her people despite the possible consequences of her actions. She asked Mordecai and all the Jews in Susa too fast for three days and nights on her behalf, saying, *"I will go to the king, even though it is against the law. And if I perish, I perish"* (Esther 4:16). The young Queen would willingly lay down her life for her people. She trusted that God would be with her when she went before the King.

After fasting and praying, she went to the king. Like someone spellbound, the moment the King laid his eyes on her, he extended his golden scepter, sparing her life (Esther 5:1-2). Instead of immediately pleading for her people, she applied wisdom. Esther invited King Xerxes and Haman to a banquet she had prepared. At the banquet, her husband asked her to demand anything, and it would be granted. She only requested they attend another banquet (Esther 5:4-8).

This delay was a strategic move. Esther was wise to wait for the right moment to reveal Haman's plot. That night, the king could not sleep and ordered the Book of Chronicles to be read to him. He learned of Mordecai's earlier act of saving his life and realized Mordecai had not received a rewarded (Esther 6:1-3). The King called for Haman and had him honor Mordecai, the man he despised, by leading him through the city on the king's horse, saying, *"This is what is done for the man the king delights to honor!"* (Esther 6:6-11).

At the second banquet, Esther revealed her Jewish identity and exposed Haman's wicked plan to cut off her people from the land.

Turning to her husband, she said:

> "If I have found favor with you, Your Majesty, and if it pleases you, grant me my life—this is my petition. And spare my people—this is my request. For I and my people have been sold to be destroyed, killed, and annihilated. If we had merely been sold as male and female slaves, I would have kept quiet, because no such distress would justify disturbing the king." (Esther 7:3-4)

King Xerxes was shocked and enraged that anyone would dare do such a thing. He asked Esther who the unfortunate soul was, and she pointed to Haman (Esther 7:5-6).

Esther and Mordecai were part of God's larger plan to protect and deliver the Jewish people from destruction. After Esther revealed Haman's plot, King Xerxes ordered Haman to hang from the gallows he had prepared for Mordecai (Esther 7:9-10). The king issued a new decree allowing the Jews to defend themselves against their enemies (Esther 8:11). On the day the enemies had hoped to overpower the Jews, the tables had turned. The Jews gained the upper hand over those who hated them (Esther 9:1).

As the issue with Haman died down, Esther's uncle, Mordecai, was elevated to a position of high honor, and the Jewish people were saved from their enemies. They celebrated the festival of Purim to celebrate their deliverance (Esther 9:20-22).

Lessons for Today

Ruth's vow to Naomi proved her deep love and compassion for her mother-in-law. She was willing to leave everything behind to support Naomi in her time of need, which was an incredibly selfless act. Like Ruth, Esther was also selfless. She risked her life to save her people from destruction. Her love for her people was greater than her fear of death. True love is sacrificial and more than mere words. You must act it out. Don't worry. It will be easy if your feelings are genuine. You should be willing to put the needs of others before yours.

Ruth, as a Moabite widow, had every right to return to her people and start a new life after her husband's death. Yet, she chose to travel with Naomi to a land she knew nothing about and live among people she had never seen. Ruth was indeed a woman of faith. Esther said, *"If I perish, I perish..."* with a heart determined to deliver her people. She was a woman of great faith. Faith in God is the fastest way to gain victory over a situation. 1 John 5:14 says, *"For everyone born of God overcomes the world. This is the victory that has overcome the world, even our faith."*

Ruth and Esther were empaths. Their compassion for others led to their upliftment. As an empath, you don't only feel for others. You act on their behalf.

A leader is not a loud and obnoxious person in a group. No. A leader is someone with quiet strength, good intentions, strategic thinking skills, courageous, and wise. Ruth and Esther were leaders who conquered all with love and compassion.

Journaling Prompt

Create a journal entry listing acts of kindness for the next three days. Aim to commit to these, journal daily, and track how you feel.

Chapter 5: Spiritual Lessons from the Psalms

What comes to your mind when you hear the word Psalms? A song? King David? If you thought of these, you have a good idea of what a psalm is about. However, a psalm could be a hymn, a poem, a prayer, or a song.

The book of Psalms comprises many songs and prayers encouraging people to praise God.[13]

Many songwriters today get inspiration for songs from the book of Psalms. Yes. There is a whole book filled with Psalms. Most chapters in the book were written by a man after God's own heart, King David. Many secrets were shared, mysteries unveiled, and prophecies told. The book of Psalms is highly spiritual. In Colossian 3:16, Paul speaks to the believers:

> *"Let the message of Christ dwell among you richly as you teach and admonish one another with all wisdom through psalms, hymns, and songs from the Spirit, singing to God with gratitude in your hearts."*

Are you looking for words of wisdom? You won't be disappointed. Are you looking for instructions? The Psalms have plenty. Are you looking for unique songs to praise and worship God? Just sit with the book of Psalms.

The book of Psalms comprises many songs and prayers encouraging people to praise God. It speaks of God's greatness and the wonderful things He has done. Psalms tells of God's faithfulness, especially during challenging times. The book reminds God's people that His Word should be at the center of their lives.

This chapter breaks from studying Biblical characters and explores the rich spiritual insights in the book of Psalms. Insights that will guide you to build a strong and resilient spiritual foundation.

The Book of Psalms is one of the most cherished books of the Bible. It often gets referred to as the "heart of the Bible." The book is a collection of songs, prayers, and hymns written by several authors anointed by God. You probably didn't know this before – one of the most popular writers is King David. Other writers include Moses and Asaph, the descendants of Korah, King Solomon, and Ethan and Heman, the Ezrahites.

This chapter aims to inspire women to deepen their relationship with God through the wisdom, prayer, and praise encapsulated in the Psalms. As you read, you will find practical ways to apply the Psalms' teachings to your daily life for spiritual growth and strength.

The Significance of the Psalms

Throughout Psalms, there is a clear picture of how God lovingly guides His people, always showing them the right path. The writers of these songs were always ready to praise and worship God. Every page in the book of Psalms is laced with strong love and devotion to God, and there are many moments in which they express their deep trust and joy in Him.

Initially titled Tehillim, which means "praise songs" in Hebrew, the book expresses a wide range of human emotions and spiritual experiences. It is composed of 150 psalms. King David is credited with writing many of them. The Psalms hold a special place in the hearts of believers. People across cultures and ages have learned to effectively speak the language of prayer and worship through their fellowship with the book of Psalms. It has proven a source of comfort, guidance, and strength for people seeking a closer relationship with God.

Every aspect of human life, from joy and praise to despair and repentance, makes them deeply relevant to personal spiritual development. As Psalm 119:105 says, "Your word is a lamp to my feet and a light to my path." The Psalms offer insight and direction to help believers navigate this tricky thing called life and the challenges within, and they present an opportunity for spiritual growth.

Key Themes in the Psalms

Trusting in God

One prominent theme in the book of Psalms is trust in God. Finding more peace in life, reducing stress, especially as a woman, and completely trusting God are the most important things you can do. Trusting people can be difficult because they often disappoint. Psalms 146:3 says, *"Do not put your trust in princes, in human beings, who cannot save."*

The world is full of uncertainties and challenges, so it is difficult to rely on it for comfort or security. However, with God, it's like lying in your mother's pouch like a baby kangaroo. You are shielded and kept safe. Throughout the Bible, God repeatedly asks believers to put their trust in Him alone. Fun fact: It was not only a suggestion. This command comes from God's deep desire for your well-being. He wants to ensure you're doing great.

Trusting God is a wise decision. You feel much closer to Him, giving you the strength to face whatever comes your way. Doubts are normal, but your new normal can be knowing that God understands your nature, your struggle with fear and worry about the future, and trusting Him instead.

There is a recurring message throughout the Psalms – whenever you feel overwhelmed by stress, remember to turn to God and trust in His plan for you. His unchanging nature and steadfast love make Him the most trustworthy. Psalm 56:3-4 says, *"When I am afraid, I put my trust in you. In God, whose word I praise—in God I trust and am not afraid. What can mere mortals do to me?"* The more you read His Word, especially the Psalms, you will find comfort in knowing God is always with you, guiding and loving you unconditionally.

For study purposes, here are 10 Psalms proving you can trust God entirely. You can read them whenever you feel your faith is wavering.

- Psalm 11
- Psalm 16
- Psalm 23
- Psalm 27
- Psalm 62
- Psalm 63
- Psalm 91
- Psalm 121
- Psalm 125
- Psalm 131

Worship

Many praise and adoration expressions for God speak of His greatness, mercy, and power in the Psalms. It contains poems and prayers promoting the worship of God in every circumstance, whether overjoyed or weighed down by sorrow. Worship is about opening your heart to God and recognizing His majesty and glory.

The Bible often refers to God as a shepherd caring for His sheep. In worship, you recognize your place before God: the sheep of His pasture. Psalm 100:3 says, *"Know that the Lord is God. It is he who made us, and we are his; we are his people, the sheep of his pasture."*

The Bible often refers to God as a shepherd caring for His sheep.[14]

You are His creation. Being dependent on His love and provision is not a crime. It is how He expects you to live. As a child of God, you cannot fully exist outside Him. Acts 17:28:

"For in him we live and move and have our being. As some of your own poets have said, We are his offspring."

The act of worship in the Psalms is deeply personal. The Psalms urges you to come before God with an open heart, offering Him praises and your whole being – your joys, sorrows, fears, and hopes. Worship is a way of life, not something you do in a church building or during a worship service. In Psalm 34:1, David declares, *"I will bless the Lord at all times; his praise shall continually be in my mouth."*

You must understand that true worship goes beyond just singing. It involves obeying God's commands and living a life reflecting His character. Worship is about aligning your life with God's will. In worship, God always uses the opportunity to transform His beloved from the inside out, so you feel different after worshiping God.

In today's world, worship helps you focus on God, especially in times of trouble or uncertainty. As you worship, you experience His presence and peace more deeply. If you haven't already, cultivate a life of worship today. You will be glad you did. Here are chapters to help you get started:

- Psalm 8
- Psalm 19
- Psalm 29
- Psalm 33
- Psalm 47
- Psalm 66
- Psalm 95
- Psalm 96
- Psalm 100
- Psalm 150

Repentance

In the book of Psalms, you encounter people who are genuinely sorry for their mistakes, asking for God's forgiveness and seeking His help. Their encounters with God often lead to genuine repentance. Through their words, you understand what it means to have a heart fully committed to God and a profound love for Him.

Repentance is about turning back to God with a humble heart and seeking His forgiveness. As Christians, recognizing your mistakes when you err and asking God for a fresh start is essential. It is easy to go off track and make choices that do not align with God's will. Fortunately, the beautiful thing about God is He is always ready to forgive and welcome His beloved back when they come to Him with a sincere heart.

You cannot overlook the theme of repentance in the Psalms. It's all over the book. King David made sure of that. The Psalms show you that repentance involves consciously turning away from sin and walking in a new direction. King David prays in Psalm 51:10, *"Create in me a pure heart, O God, and renew a steadfast spirit within me."* He knew he could trust God to help him serve Him better.

In the book of Psalms, writers openly confess their sins and seek God's forgiveness. Repentance is being honest with God. You may deceive people around you, and sometimes, even yourself, through gaslighting, but you can never deceive God. He knows you better than you know yourself. True repentance begins with acknowledging the wrong you have done.

Psalm 32:5 says:

"Then I acknowledged my sin to you and did not cover up my iniquity. I said, 'I will confess my transgressions to the Lord.' And you forgave the guilt of my sin." 1 John 1:8-9, "If we claim to be without sin, we deceive ourselves and the truth is not in us. If we confess our sins, he is faithful and just and will forgive us our sins and purify us from all unrighteousness."

You cannot live a perfect life on your own. You will always need God's help to walk in righteousness. Repentance is one way to show God you depend on Him for grace and strength. God's love is greater than your failures, and His mercy is always available when you turn to Him with a repentant heart.

- Psalm 6
- Psalm 25
- Psalm 32
- Psalm 38
- Psalm 51
- Psalm 102
- Psalm 103
- Psalm 130
- Psalm 143
- Psalm 139

Seeking God's Guidance

Life is loaded with many uncertain moments, with overwhelming choices confusing you about your next line of action. You need God's guidance. The Psalms contain prayers acting as God's hotlines when you need guidance. Psalm 25:4-5 which says:

"Show me your ways, Lord, teach me your paths. Guide me in your truth and teach me, for you are God my Savior, and my hope is in you all day long."

Why do you need God's guidance? You did not create yourself. You easily make mistakes or choose a path far from His will. The Bible says in Proverbs 14:12, *"There is a way that appears to be right, but in the end leads to death."*

In Isaiah 48:21, the Bible also talks about how God does the impossible for His people when He leads them:

"They did not thirst when he led them through the deserts; he made water flow for them from the rock; he split the rock and water gushed out."

Who wouldn't want to be led by a God like that?

"He made water flow for them from the rock."[15]

Seeking God's guidance is essential. When you allow room for God's guidance, He directs your steps. He promised in Psalms 32:8:

"I will instruct you and teach you in the way you should go; I will counsel you with my loving eye on you."

God is always ready to guide you. Please note: you don't have to wait until you're lost before asking for His guidance. He wants to be involved in every decision you make, big or small. Make seeking His guidance daily a habit, and you will see how aligned you become with His will for your life.

- Psalm 5
- Psalm 16
- Psalm 23
- Psalm 25
- Psalm 32

- Psalm 48
- Psalm 73
- Psalm 143
- Psalm 139

Psalms Offering Wisdom and Encouragement

Wisdom Psalms

- Psalm 1
- Psalm 14
- Psalm 37
- Psalm 73
- Psalm 91
- Psalm 112
- Psalm 119
- Psalm 128

Psalms of Encouragement

Sometimes, you may feel like no one understands what you're going through. You might open up to a friend or loved one, hoping their advice will help you. God understands you better than anyone else. He made provision for the Psalms to encourage you whenever you feel left out or forsaken.

Here are 20 verses of encouragement from the Psalms:

- **Psalm 37:3-4, 7:** *"Trust in the Lord and do good; dwell in the land and enjoy safe pasture. Take delight in the Lord, and he will give you the desires of your heart. ... Be still before the Lord and wait patiently for him; do not fret when people succeed in their ways when they carry out their wicked schemes."*

- **Psalm 121:1-2:** *"I lift up my eyes to the mountains—where does my help come from? My help comes from the Lord, the Maker of heaven and earth."*

- **Psalm 23:4:** *"Even though I walk through the darkest valley, I will fear no evil, for you are with me; your rod and your staff, they comfort me."*

- **Psalm 27:1:** *"The Lord is my light and my salvation—whom shall I fear? The Lord is the stronghold of my life—of whom shall I be afraid?"*
- **Psalm 28:7:** *"The Lord is my strength and my shield; my heart trusts in him, and he helps me. My heart leaps for joy, and with my song I praise him."*
- **Psalm 31:24:** *"Be strong and take heart, all you who hope in the Lord."*
- **Psalm 34:4:** *"I sought the Lord, and he answered me; he delivered me from all my fears."*
- **Psalm 34:17-18**: *"The righteous cry out, and the Lord hears them; he delivers them from all their troubles. The Lord is close to the brokenhearted."*
- **Psalm 37:4:** *"Take delight in the Lord, and he will give you the desires of your heart."*
- **Psalm 37:5:** *"Commit your way to the Lord; trust in him
- and he will do this."*
- **Psalm 46:1:** *"God is our refuge and strength, an ever-present help in trouble."*
- **Psalm 55:22:** *"Cast your cares on the Lord and he will sustain you; he will never let the righteous be shaken."*
- **Psalm 56:3:** *"When I am afraid, I put my trust in you."*
- **Psalm 61:2:** *"From the ends of the earth I call to you, I call as my heart grows faint; lead me to the rock that is higher than I."*
- **Psalm 62:6:** *"Truly he is my rock and my salvation; he is my fortress; I will not be shaken."*
- **Psalm 91:2:** *"I will say of the Lord, 'He is my refuge and my fortress, my God, in whom I trust."*
- **Psalm 91:4:** *"He will cover you with his feathers, and under his wings, you will find refuge; his faithfulness will be your shield and rampart."*
- **Psalm 94:19:** *"When anxiety was great within me, your consolation brought me joy."*

- **Psalm 118:6:** *"The Lord is with me; I will not be afraid. What can mere mortals do to me?"*
- **Psalm 30:5:** *"For his anger lasts only a moment, but his favor lasts a lifetime; weeping may stay for the night, but rejoicing comes in the morning."*

God is deeply aware of all your thoughts, actions, and needs, and His presence constantly surrounds you. The book of Psalms encourages you to live with the assurance that you are never alone.

The Importance of Prayer and Meditation

Prayer and meditation are crucial in developing a solid spiritual life. Meditation, as in the Psalms, involves deeply pondering God's Word and His works. It helps you quiet your mind, connect with God, and gain clarity and strength for your daily life.

You must willingly set aside time for prayer and meditation in your daily life. For instance, King David's secret behind his victory and successful walk with God was prayer and meditation. When you pray, you speak to God and align your mind and heart with His Spirit.

Prayer has the power to transform your life entirely. When you pray regularly, you will notice a shift in your thinking. You become more positive, patient, and understanding. This shift doesn't happen overnight. However, you can create new, healthier patterns of thought, leading to better actions with consistent effort. Prayer helps you let go of the old ways that no longer serve you and become the woman God has purposed you to be.

Like Jesus sought solitude to pray and meditate, you, too, need this quiet time to renew your spirit. Life can be overwhelming with its many demands and distractions. But when you take time to be alone with God, you hear His voice more clearly and feel His presence more profoundly.

Prayer and meditation offer a unique opportunity. Together, as a power combo, they help you let go of worries, fears, and doubts. You gain renewed purpose and direction, knowing you no longer move through life blindly because God guides you, keeping you grounded in faith.

Timeless Relevance of the Psalms

The timeless relevance of the Psalms is evident in their connection to modern spiritual practices. They have existed for countless generations, offering comfort, wisdom, and inspiration. As you turn to a friend for advice or a shoulder to cry on, you can turn to the Psalms for guidance and solace.

The Psalms are incredibly relatable. Whether you feel overwhelmed, lost, or need a connection with something greater than yourself, the Psalms offer a comforting and familiar presence. They can help you express your deepest feelings to God. Sometimes, finding the right words to convey what's happening inside you is challenging. The Psalms provide a language allowing you to pour your heart out to the Lord your God.

The book of Psalms offers a timeless source of comfort, wisdom, and guidance. The more you study and use the Psalms, the more you deepen your connection with God and become empowered to live a more fulfilling life.

Journaling Prompt

Create a personal Psalm in your journal. Reflect on your spiritual journey and write a Psalm that expresses your prayers, praises, and reflections to God, inspired by the style and themes of the Biblical Psalms.

Chapter 6: Getting Closer to God Through the Gospels

Bible study aims to help you connect with God more profoundly. The entire sixty-six books of the Bible are God's attempt to bring Himself closer to His people. From the Old Testament to the New Testament, believers can experience God through numerous bible stories and understand how faithful He is to those He calls his own.

Since the beginning of this book, the Bible characters studied were from the Old Testament. Women who had never met Jesus nor His disciples yet still believed in the God of their fathers. The people of the Old Testament had no one to bring them the good news, but like Joshua, they and their households could choose to serve the Lord even amid confusion.

The New Testament is rich with Jesus' teachings and stories in the Gospels.[16]

This chapter centers on deepening and nurturing your relationship with God through Jesus' teachings and stories in the Gospels. So, it is time to explore books in the New Testament. This chapter aims to inspire you to follow the examples of Jesus and his disciples, fostering a closer and more personal connection with God.

The word *gospel* is derived from the Old English *Godspell*, which translates from the Greek word *euangelion*, meaning *good news* or *good telling*. This word described important news, like when a king won a battle or something good happened in the kingdom. The meaning of the word *gospel* became much deeper when Jesus came, over 400 years after the last book of the Old Testament was written. It became the perfect word for the special message Jesus brought to the world.

The Messiah came with a message of hope for people who felt lost or without help. He came to bring freedom to those who were suffering or feeling trapped. So, the word *gospel* became closely linked with the story of Jesus. Jesus and his disciples left the body of Christ with many interactions and examples to help shape the believers' minds into one fit for a glorious life with God.

The Core Teachings of the Gospels

The Gospels are the books in the Bible that tell about the life and ministry of Jesus. They were written to teach and show believers who Jesus was, what He did, and why He came. The Gospels center around the good news Jesus Christ came to share with the entire world. What was this good news? It is the message about God's unending love for mankind and how they could have a close relationship with Him.

Each Gospel provides a unique view of Jesus' life, His teachings, His miracles, and His compassion for people. The Gospels are the four accounts written by Jesus' disciples. It made sense to call them "Gospels" because they all shared the same good news that Jesus came to bring.

The first four books of the New Testament, Matthew, Mark, Luke, and John, are like four windows offering an insider's perspective of Jesus' life from different angles. Each highlights various aspects of Jesus' life and ministry, but they all portray his love for people and his desire to bring them closer to God.

Key Moments in Jesus' Ministry

The Sermon on the Mount

The sermon beginning with a blessing is God's way of assuring you of His unwavering promise of blessing. The aim is to remind you of His intention to bless you and His unfailing promises.

The Sermon on the Mount is in the book of Matthew, from chapter 5 to chapter 7. It was Jesus' longest teaching in the Gospels. The sermon laid out Jesus' moral vision for humanity. Jesus teaches a large crowd how to live if they want to follow God. He centered on humility, compassion, and forgiveness.

The sermon starts with the Beatitudes, a series of blessings describing the attitudes and actions that please God.

Matthew 5:1-12:

> *"Now when Jesus saw the crowds, he went up on a mountainside and sat down. His disciples came to him, and he began to teach them. He said: "Blessed are the poor in spirit, for theirs is the kingdom of heaven. Blessed are those who mourn, for they will be comforted. Blessed are the meek, for they will inherit the earth. Blessed are those who hunger and thirst for righteousness, for they will be filled. Blessed are the merciful, for they will be shown mercy. Blessed are the pure in heart, for they will see God. Blessed are the peacemakers, for they will be called children of God. Blessed are those who are persecuted because of righteousness, for theirs is the kingdom of heaven. Blessed are you when people insult you, persecute you, and falsely say all kinds of evil against you because of me. Rejoice and be glad because great is your reward in heaven, for in the same way they persecuted the prophets who were before you."*

Beatitudes means a state of supreme happiness. So, this first part of the sermon was Jesus teaching the people that true happiness comes from living in a way that is pleasing to God. These mental states of mind became the blueprint for all who would become His disciples.

As He continued, Jesus referred to the believer as the light in a world of darkness and as the salt adding taste to the world around them:

"You are the salt of the earth. But if the salt loses its saltiness, how can it be made salty again? It is no longer good for anything except to be thrown out and trampled underfoot. You are the light of the world. A town built on a hill cannot be hidden. Neither do people light a lamp and put it under a bowl. Instead, they put it on its stand, and it gives light to everyone in the house. In the same way, let your light shine before others, that they may see your good deeds and glorify your Father in heaven." Matthew 5:13-16

He further tells them about acceptably fulfilling the law. He gave them a deeper understanding of God's commandments concerning murder (Matthew 5:21-25), adultery (Matthew 5:27-30), divorce (Matthew 5:31-32), oaths (Matthew 5:33-37), and vengeance (an eye for an eye) (Matthew 5:38-42).

Jesus taught that it is not enough to avoid murdering someone. He explained that if you are angry with someone without a good reason, you have broken the commandment because of murder in your heart.

Speaking on adultery, He said even looking at a person with lust is committing adultery in your heart. He admonished Christians to control what they do, think, and feel.

Think of what the world would be like if people truly obeyed these teachings, not only in their actions but also in their hearts. It would be like heaven. There would be no road rage, no shouting matches, no malice, no unnecessary violence, and no harsh words hurting others. People would be more patient and understanding and work hard to solve problems peacefully.

Instead of winning arguments, they would focus on finding solutions and making peace. If the commandment against lust were obeyed in spirit, there would be no infidelity, and marriages would be stronger and happier. Families would be more stable, and children would grow up in loving homes. There would be no need for pornography, etc. The industry would run out of business instead of flourishing like today. The world would be a much better place if everyone lived according to the law's spirit.

Jesus says to love those who mistreat you, forgive them, and pray for them.[17]

Also, Jesus gave the most difficult instructions to follow: *"Love your enemies"* (Matthew 5:44) and *"Be perfect, just as your Father in heaven is perfect"* (Matthew 5:48). God is perfect because God is love. Usually, when people are hurt, their first reaction is to hurt their offenders back or hold a grudge. However, Jesus says to love those who mistreat you, forgive them, and pray for them. This love is not easy, but it is the love God shows to all people.

God's love is unconditional. He cares deeply for everyone, even those who do not believe in Him or respect His name. He loves those who reject Him or use His name in vain. His love is not based on what you do or don't do. His love stems from His character and desire for everyone to know Him.

In Matthew 6, Jesus shifted the focus to trusting God and seeking His kingdom first. He tells the people not to worry about their daily needs, like food and clothing, because God knows what they need and will provide. He says, *"Seek first the kingdom of God and His righteousness, and all these things will be added to you"* Matthew 6:33.

Remember how the Bible says in Psalms 23:1, *"The Lord is my shepherd, I lack nothing,"* Psalms 34:10 says, *"The lions may grow weak and hungry, but those who seek the LORD lack no good thing."* Jesus was merely establishing what had been said centuries before Him. It shows that God is indeed faithful. When you seek and trust Him, He will bless you with every good thing.

The sermon included a session on being sincere in your actions and not only doing things to look good in front of others. Jesus talks about giving to the needy, praying, and fasting privately rather than doing these things to show off. God looks at the heart, and He values genuine devotion over outward appearances, 1 Samuel 16:17:

> *"But the LORD said unto Samuel, "Look not on his countenance or on the height of his stature, because I have refused him; for the LORD seeth not as man seeth. For man looketh on the outward appearance, but the LORD looketh on the heart."*

When you do good things quietly and sincerely, without seeking praise from others, it indicates your love for God is real and you are more concerned about what God thinks than what people think.

The Sermon on the Mount provides many lessons on how to live a life that is pleasing to God. You will learn to become humbler, loving, forgiving, and sincere if you study and meditate on it. You will grow closer to God and live in a way that reflects His love and righteousness.

Famous Parables

Jesus was famously known for speaking in *parables* in public places. It usually left the people confused. He did his best to explain them without using complex words. His disciples also had problems understanding His parables. So, He took His time to break it down, saying, *"...Because the knowledge of the secrets of the kingdom of heaven has been given to you, but not to them."* (Matthew 13:11).

But what does a parable mean? A parable is a simple story using everyday situations to illustrate a more profound spiritual truth. Some of the most famous parables Jesus told include:

The Parable of the Good Samaritan (Luke 10:29-37)

"But he wanted to justify himself, so he asked Jesus, "And who is my neighbor?" In reply, Jesus said: "A man was going down from Jerusalem to Jericho when he was attacked by robbers. They stripped him of his clothes, beat him, and went away, leaving him half dead. A priest happened to be going down the same road, and when he saw the man, he passed by on the other side. So, too, a Levite, when he came to the place and saw him, passed by on the other side. But a Samaritan, as he traveled, came where the man was; and when he saw him, he took pity on him. He went to him and bandaged his wounds, pouring on oil and wine. Then he put the man on his own donkey, brought him to an inn, and took care of him. The next day he took out two denarii and gave them to the innkeeper. 'Look after him,' he said, 'and when I return, I will reimburse you for any extra expense you may have.' "Which of these three do you think was a neighbor to the man who fell into the hands of robbers?" The expert in the law replied, "The one who had mercy on him." Jesus told him, "Go and do likewise."

In this story, a man is traveling from Jerusalem to Jericho when he is attacked by robbers, beaten, and left for dead. Several people pass by without helping him. Finally, a Samaritan — a person from Samaria whom the Jews did not like — bandages the man's wounds, takes him to an inn, and pays for his care. Jesus told this parable to encourage believers to act lovingly and caringly show kindness, compassion, and mercy to everyone because true neighborliness comes from the heart.

The Parable of the Prodigal Son (Luke 15:11-32)

"Jesus continued: "There was a man who had two sons. The younger one said to his father, 'Father, give me my share of the estate.' So, he divided his property between them. Not long after that, the younger son got together all he had, set off for a distant country and there squandered his wealth in wild living. After he had spent everything, there was a severe famine in that whole country, and he began to be in need. So, he went and hired himself out to a citizen of that country, who sent him to his fields to feed pigs. He longed to fill his stomach with the pods that the pigs were eating, but

no one gave him anything. When he came to his senses, he said, 'How many of my father's hired servants have food to spare, and here I am starving to death! I will set out and go back to my father and say to him: Father, I have sinned against heaven and against you. I am no longer worthy to be called your son; make me like one of your hired servants.' So, he got up and went to his father. But while he was still a long way off, his father saw him and was filled with compassion for him; he ran to his son, threw his arms around him, and kissed him. The son said to him, 'Father, I have sinned against heaven and against you. I am no longer worthy to be called your son.' But the father said to his servants, 'Quick! Bring the best robe and put it on him. Put a ring on his finger and sandals on his feet. Bring the fattened calf and kill it. Let's have a feast and celebrate. For this son of mine was dead and is alive again; he was lost and is found.' So, they began to celebrate. Meanwhile, the older son was in the field. When he came near the house, he heard music and dancing. So, he called one of the servants and asked him what was going on. 'Your brother has come,' he replied, 'and your father has killed the fattened calf because he has him back safe and sound.' The older brother became angry and refused to go in. So, his father went out and pleaded with him. But he answered his father, 'Look! All these years I've been slaving for you and never disobeyed your orders. Yet you never gave me even a young goat so I could celebrate with my friends. But when this son of yours who has squandered your property with prostitutes comes home, you kill the fattened calf for him!' My son,' the father said, 'you are always with me, and everything I have is yours. But we had to celebrate and be glad because this brother of yours was dead and is alive again; he was lost and is found."

    Like most people, the prodigal son wanted to live independently of his father. Jesus told this story to help people understand the depth of God's love. It didn't matter how long the son was gone, what he did with his father's money, or how he looked when he returned. His father readily received him with open arms and a kiss.

    In the parable, the prodigal son represents people who have journeyed on their own, far from God. The father represents God, who is unconditional in His love. A God willing to accept you whenever you acknowledge your mistakes and return to Him. 1 John 1:9, "If we confess our sins, he is faithful and just and will forgive us our sins and purify us from all unrighteousness." Malachi 3:7:

> *"Ever since the time of your ancestors you have turned away from my decrees and have not kept them. Return to me, and I will return to you," says the Lord Almighty."*

The Parable of the Lost Sheep (Luke 15:1-7)

> *"Now the tax collectors and sinners were all gathering around to hear Jesus. 2 But the Pharisees and the teachers of the law muttered, "This man welcomes sinners and eats with them." Then Jesus told them this parable: "Suppose one of you has a hundred sheep and loses one of them. Doesn't he leave the ninety-nine in the open country and go after the lost sheep until he finds it? And when he finds it, he joyfully puts it on his shoulders and goes home. Then he calls his friends and neighbors together and says, 'Rejoice with me; I have found my lost sheep.' I tell you that in the same way, there will be more rejoicing in heaven over one sinner who repents than over ninety-nine righteous persons who do not need to repent."*

Jesus used this parable to explain how important every soul is to God. Leaving an entire flock of sheep to chase after one is not something many would do. But God is not man. He doesn't think like one. He wants all sinners to repent and draw close to Him. The Lord said in Ezekiel 18:23:

> *"Do I take any pleasure in the death of the wicked? Declares the Sovereign Lord. Rather, am I not pleased when they turn from their ways and live?"*

Jesus used the lost sheep parable to explain how important every soul is to God.[18]

He was immensely fond of King David because, while tending to his father's sheep, David would chase and kill wild animals that tried to take his sheep. He could have run back home to tell his father that the lion and the bear attacked them. Instead, he kept the rest safe and chased after the animals because of one sheep. God loves all His children, and His mercy endures forever. Isaiah 43:4 says:

> *"Since you are precious and honored in my sight, and because I love you, I will give people in exchange for you, nations in exchange for your life."*

King David wrote a Psalm on God's love:

> *"Give thanks to the Lord, for he is good. His love endures forever. Give thanks to the God of gods. His love endures forever..."* Psalm 136

These are a few parables Jesus told. You can study many more during your Bible study.

- Parable of the Sower (Mark 4:1-20)
- Parable of the Pharisee and Publican (Luke 18:9-14)
- Parable of the Mustard Seed (Matthew 13:31-32)
- Parable of the Ten Virgins (Matthew 25:1-13)
- Parable of the Lost Coin (Luke 15:8-10)
- Parable of the Talents (Matthew 25:14-30)

Notable Miracles

The Feeding of the Five Thousand (Matthew 14:13-21)

The four gospels recount a miracle where Jesus fed five thousand people with only five loaves of bread and two fish. It was such a dramatic day. One moment, the disciples were anxious and worrying about how to feed the multitude. A thanksgiving prayer with five loaves of bread and two fishes later, Jesus performed a miracle.

Everyone ate until full, and there were leftovers. The disciples couldn't believe their eyes. This miracle was Jesus' way of showing the people that nothing was impossible with God. In Psalm 78:22-24, King David testified of God's ability to perform a miracle like this:

> *"...for they did not believe in God or trust in his deliverance. Yet he gave a command to the skies above and opened the doors of the heavens; he rained down manna for the people*

to eat, he gave them the grain of heaven." Read the original story in Exodus 16.

Always have faith in God's provision and be willing to share what you have. God can multiply your small offerings to meet greater needs in the blink of an eye. Matthew 19:26, *"...With man this is impossible, but with God all things are possible."*

Jesus Walking on Water (Matthew 14:22-32)

Have you ever looked at the ocean? Have you truly observed the ocean and watched how the water moves? What about its depth? Have you ever thought about the depth of an ocean? Water is larger than the entire land area on Earth. Water holds immense energy when it flows, which is called kinetic energy. Researchers learned that water covers over 70 percent of the Earth's surface, and 96.5 percent is seawater.

Now, with this context in mind, picture Jesus walking on water - not a fountain, a stream, a lake, or a river, but a sea. A sea! He did so with a calm and unbothered demeanor. He walked majestically like the King He is. He could have even been reading a scroll as He walked, paying no mind to the sea, only looking up to see He was on the right path to the boat as if it was an everyday activity. He asked Peter to come to Him, and Peter walked water until he allowed fear to cloud his mind.

With his unshakable faith in God, Jesus walked on water.[19]

This miracle happened after the feeding of the five thousand. Jesus sent His disciples ahead in a boat while He went up a mountain to pray. The disciples' boat was far from land during the night, and the wind was strong. Jesus came to them, walking on the water. The disciples were terrified, thinking He was a ghost, but Jesus reassured them, saying, *"Take courage! It is I. Don't be afraid."*

When Peter began to sink, Jesus reached out and caught him, saying, *"You of little faith, why did you doubt?"* Faith helps you overcome fear; however, it disguises itself. This miracle shows that Jesus will always help when you call out to Him.

The Woman with a Blood Issue

The story of the woman with the issue of blood is in three of the four gospels. This woman had suffered from this health challenge for over twelve years. Unlike the man at the pool of Bethesda, who had no one, the woman had people and money. She had been to the hospital several times, and presumably, doctors avoided her. Seeing a patient suffering from an illness you've tried over and over to cure is like a blow to your profession.

The woman spent all her money and time for more than 12 years looking for a solution to her predicament. All efforts were fruitless. One day, she heard Jesus was visiting the house of a synagogue leader in her area. She said to herself, *"If I just touch his clothes, I will be healed."* The miracle happened the moment she touched His garment. Suddenly, the blood dried up, and she was free.

Jesus felt power leave His body, and He perceived that someone with faith had touched Him – faith that was hard to ignore. He turned and asked, *"Who touched my clothes?"* But his disciples answered that it could have been anyone because a large crowd followed them. However, Jesus was no ordinary man. He knew it was someone special and kept looking.

The woman realized He would search until He found her, so she presented herself to Him. Jesus looked at her and smiled. He said to her, *"Daughter, your faith has healed you. Go in peace and be freed from your suffering."* This marked the end of her predicament.

What is that issue causing you heartache and distress? It doesn't matter how long or what the doctors call it. Jesus can heal you. Reach out to Him in faith today and receive your healing. In Isaiah 53:4, Prophet Isaiah prophesied about Jesus:

"Surely, he took up our pain and bore our suffering, yet we considered him punished by God, stricken by him, and afflicted. But he was pierced for our transgressions, he was crushed for our iniquities; the

punishment that brought us peace was on him, and by his wounds we are healed."

There are many other miracles in the gospels like these. Here are some you can study and meditate on later:

- The healing of the man born blind (John 9:1-12)
- The man at the pool of Bethesda (John 5:1-15)
- Turning water into wine (John 2:1-11)
- Raising Lazarus from the dead (John 11:1-43)
- Calming the storm (Mark 4:35-41)

Through these miracles, Jesus reveals the compassionate and powerful nature of God. When Jesus heals the sick, feeds the hungry, or raises the dead, He demonstrates His divine power and displays how active God is in the lives of those who trust and believe in Him.

Love, Compassion, and Forgiveness: Central Themes in the Gospels

In drawing closer to God, you cannot overemphasize the love, compassion, and forgiveness. Jesus admonishes believers to love each other as He loves them in John 13:34. Love is a spiritual force keeping God close to you. Chapter 4, on love and compassion, had more to say about this with scriptures and Bible characters who were agents of love and compassion.

Kindness or compassion is about noticing when someone needs help and helping them like Jesus did. It is not about noticing a problem and then going home to gossip about it with your friends. From the story of the Good Samaritan, you can see genuine kindness goes beyond what's typical or expected. The Good Samaritan helped a hurt stranger, even though they weren't of the same social status or culture. Showing kindness to loved ones and strangers is one way to live a Godly life, the life Christ lived.

Regarding forgiveness, Jesus teaches that you must forgive others to receive God's forgiveness (Matthew 6:14-15). Forgiveness frees you from the burden of bitterness and allows you to experience the fullness of God's grace. You feel lighter and more peaceful the moment you let go of anger or hurt. You reflect God's forgiving nature, which opens the door for deeper communion with Him if you practice forgiveness.

The Model for Discipleship and Spiritual Growth

Jesus' interactions with His disciples provide a model for discipleship and spiritual growth. He taught them through His words and by His example. He demonstrated how to live obediently to God, serve others, and remain faithful even in challenges. He imbibed in them the vital characteristics of true leadership: service, humility, and love.

Jesus called them to be with Him, to learn from Him, and to support one another. They were His family, friends, and community. A community like that is essential for nurturing a relationship with God because it provides encouragement, accountability, and a shared faith experience. So, even as you pursue spiritual growth, keep room for creating or joining a community that loves God like you do. You can learn from each other's experiences and encounters with God.

Journaling Prompt

Create a weekly devotion plan based on the Gospels. Each day, read a passage from the Gospels you wrote about in your journal (make it stand out by adding creativity), reflect on its meaning, and write down how you can apply it to your life. Use this practice to nurture and strengthen your relationship with God.

Chapter 7: Women of the Gospel: The Stories of Mary and Mary Magdalene

After exploring the four gospels, it is a good time to read stories of notable women of the gospels. Unlike the Old Testament, which referred to many women and their impact on God's purpose for the Israelites, the New Testament only mentions a few.

The New Testament celebrated more men than women – Jesus' closest disciples were men. However, whenever a crowd listened to Jesus, the women were more in attendance than men, which is still evident today. If you enter a well-populated church, you will notice most members are women. They may not always take up a leadership role – but they are always present where Jesus is.

The New Testament also tells stories of two women who stood out in Jesus' ministry.[20]

This character-based chapter focuses on the stories and profiles of two women who stood out in Jesus' ministry – how they met Him, grew in faith as they listened to His teachings, became disciples and loyal followers, and followed Him until His death and after His resurrection.

More interestingly, they have the same name. You've probably guessed it already. So, are you down for more Bible character study? If yes, then keep reading.

Mary | The Mother of Jesus

Mary, the mother of Jesus, was an average young lady next door – quiet, calm, beautiful, kept to herself, and faithful to God and her fiancé. When Mary got engaged, she was still a virgin and an exemplary, nice young woman. Many men clamored to woo her. However, the lucky man was Joseph, a decent, humble, and God-fearing man.

Joseph came from King David's lineage, born and raised in a small town of Nazareth in Galilee. His ancestors were Abraham, Isaac, Jacob, Judah, Jesse, etc. He had a high-paying job in carpentry and was comfortably well-off. Unlike some of the men in the town, he didn't want to fool around with just any woman. He knew Mary was the one for him and wanted to make her an honest wife.

Their relationship was the talk of the town. They were perfect for each other. However, Joseph made a shocking discovery with the wedding date approaching fast. Mary was pregnant! His virgin fiancée was pregnant.

How did this happen? The Book of Luke records that the angel Gabriel visited Mary. Luke 1:26-35,:

> *"The angel came to her and said, "You are honored very much. You are a favored woman. The Lord is with you. You are chosen from among many women." When she saw the angel, she was troubled by his words. She thought about what had been said. The angel said to her, "Mary, do not be afraid. You have found favor with God. See! You are to become a mother and have a Son. You are to give Him the name Jesus. He will be great. He will be called the Son of the Most High. The Lord God will give Him the place where His early father David sat. He will be King over the family of Jacob forever and His nation will have no end." Mary said to the angel, "How will this happen? I have never*

had a man." The angel said to her, "The Holy Spirit will come on you. The power of the Most High will cover you. The holy Child you give birth to will be called the Son of God."

Although shocked and confused, Mary, as always, willingly served God's purpose. Her heart raced when the angel left her. How would she tell Joseph? What would she tell him? What about her family? Joseph's family? How could she explain becoming pregnant overnight? What does she tell her best friend? The questions kept rolling through her mind, but then she remembered the word of the Lord from the angel: *"Do not be afraid. You have found favor with God."*

So, Mary steeled herself and kept her emotions in check. God would not put her to shame. She knew Him as faithful and just. Even though she was young, she had dedicated her life to serving the Lord. God heard her thoughts and noted her worries, so he sent an angel to speak to Joseph.

Joseph, respecting the laws of the land prepared to break the engagement. The child was not his, so he shouldn't be the one marrying Mary. He decided to do it quietly so as to not hurt Mary's image. While planning to let her go, an angel visited him in a dream and explained the situation. Matthew 1:20-21:

> *"While he was thinking about this, an angel of the Lord came to him in a dream. The angel said, "Joseph, son of David, do not be afraid to take Mary as your wife. She is to become a mother by the Holy Spirit. A Son will be born to her. You will give Him the name Jesus because He will save His people from the punishment of their sins."*

After the angel's visit, Joseph knew what to do. He quickly married Mary and assisted her throughout the pregnancy. Mary thanks God for choosing her in Luke 1:46-55:

> *"Then Mary said, "My heart sings with thanks for my Lord. And my spirit is happy in God, the One Who saves from the punishment of sin. The Lord has looked on me, His servant-girl and one who is not important. But from now on all people will honor me. He Who is powerful has done great things for me. His name is Holy. The loving-kindness of the Lord is given to the people of all times who honor Him. He has done powerful works with His arm. He has divided from*

each other those who have pride in their hearts. He has taken rulers down from their thrones. He has put those who are in a place that is not important to a place that is important. He has filled those who are hungry with good things. He has sent the rich people away with nothing. He has helped Israel His servant. This was done to remember His loving-kindness. He promised He would do this to our early fathers and to Abraham and to his family forever."

After seeing that God had opened Elizabeth's womb like the angel said, reality dawned on Mary, and she couldn't contain her joy.

When Jesus started His ministry at the wedding in Cana, Mary told the servants, *"Whatever He tells you, do it"* John 2:5. Mary knew exactly who Jesus was and what He could do. He did not disappoint.

When Jesus' ministry on Earth ended, it was time to say goodbye to his human form at the cross. Mary was gripped with grief. She had watched Him grow from a tiny baby wrapped in swaddling clothes to the wounded and bruised man hanging on the cross as was prophesied about Him. Mary was sad but grateful. God's will be done, and she had played her part in it.

Mary Magdalene | The Woman Disciple

Mary Magdalene is another Mary featured in Jesus' life, and her presence wasn't fleeting. She was first introduced in Luke 8:1-3, *"After this, Jesus traveled about from one town and village to another, proclaiming the good news of the kingdom of God. The Twelve were with him, and also some women who had been cured of evil spirits and diseases: Mary (called Magdalene) from whom seven demons had come out; Joanna, the wife of Chuza, the manager of Herod's household; Susanna; and many others. These women were helping to support them out of their own means."*

Mary Magdalene, a close follower of Jesus, loved and believed in Him immensely.[21]

The Bible records that she was one of the women who traveled with Jesus and supported His ministry with her finances. All the gospels had something to say about her because of her dedication and activeness in Jesus' ministry.

Mary Magdalene, a close follower of Jesus, loved and believed in Him immensely. At Jesus' crucifixion, she was there. It was sad and heartbreaking because Jesus, who had taught much about love and kindness, was treated so cruelly. Most people who gathered at the cross to witness the crucifixion left the scene after a while, but Mary stayed because she wanted to be close to Jesus. She witnessed His suffering until He died. Standing near the cross, Mary watched Jesus speak His last words. She saw the sky turn dark, felt the earth shake, and experienced everything that happened afterward.

When soldiers came to take Jesus' body away, she made sure to locate where He was buried. She and other women wanted to ensure His body was cared for, so they planned to return back after the Sabbath. Early Sunday morning, while it was still dark, Mary Magdalene went to the tomb. She wanted to put special spices on Jesus' body, as was the custom. When she arrived, Mary saw the huge stone covering the tomb's entrance had rolled away! Confused and thinking someone might have taken Jesus' body, she ran to tell the disciples, Peter and John. They came to see for themselves.

As she wept, Mary looked into the tomb again. This time, she saw two angels dressed in white sitting where Jesus' body had been. They asked her:

"Why are you crying?"

She answered:

"They have taken my Lord away, and I don't know where they have put Him."

Then she turned around and saw a man standing there whom she thought was a gardener (John 20:13-14).

Then, the man said her name, "Mary." At that moment, Mary realized it was Jesus speaking. He was alive! Her heart must have leaped with joy. Jesus told her to go and tell the others that He had risen from the dead. Mary Magdalene ran to tell the disciples the amazing news. She couldn't wait to share that Jesus had risen like He said He would. She was the first person to see Jesus alive. She was so excited to share this miracle with everyone.

There is a common misconception about Mary Magdalene being a prostitute. The Bible does not explicitly say that Mary Magdalene was a prostitute. It only records the one time when Jesus cast out seven demons from her (Luke 8:2). Some people believe Mary Magdalene was the same person as another unnamed woman in the Bible, who many thought was a prostitute and is known for washing Jesus' feet with her tears and drying them with her hair (Luke 7:36-38). However, there is no evidence that these two women are the same person.

Lessons from Their Lives

Faith and Obedience

Mary demonstrated deep faith and obedience by accepting God's will for her life, even when facing uncertainty and potential shame. Her response to angel Gabriel's message was trust and submission, saying, *"I am the Lord's servant...May your word to me be fulfilled"* (Luke 1:38). She accepted her role as Jesus' mother, trusting in God's plan despite the challenges that would come with it. Her faith was steadfast, and she remained obedient to God's call. Mary became the perfect example of trusting God's purpose, even when you do not fully understand the circumstances.

Mary Magdalene's faith and obedience were evident in her unwavering support for Jesus throughout His ministry. Mary Magdalene followed Jesus faithfully despite her past, providing for Him and His disciples. She embraced her role with devotion. Her faith led to her transformation and a new purpose.

Courage and Perseverance

Mary, Jesus' mother, showed immense courage when she accepted the angel's message that she would bear the Son of God. She faced potential disgrace, misunderstanding, and rejection from her community, yet she willingly obeyed God. She persevered through her personal pain, trusting in God's greater plan.

Mary, Jesus' mother, showed immense courage when she accepted the angel's message that she would bear the Son of God.[22]

Mary Magdalene's courage is highlighted by her presence at Jesus' crucifixion when many others fled in fear. She persevered in her devotion to Jesus, even when He was no longer physically present. She displayed courage by going to the tomb to honor Jesus' body. She did not let fear or societal judgment deter her from her devotion.

Devotion and Service

Virgin Mary's devotion is seen throughout Jesus' life, from His birth to His death. She cared for Him, supported His ministry, and followed Him to the very end. She was wholly humble with a profound purpose. Even at the wedding in Cana, she demonstrated her faith in Jesus by encouraging others to follow His instructions, showing her ongoing devotion and service to His mission.

Mary Magdalene's devotion is evident in her financial support of Jesus' ministry and constant presence with Him. She followed Jesus and served His mission actively, providing for Him and His disciples. Her devotion was unwavering, and she was among the first to witness His resurrection. She was entrusted with the task of delivering the news to the disciples.

Witness and Proclamation

Mary, Jesus' mother, was crucial as a witness to Jesus' life, death, and resurrection. She witnessed Jesus' first miracle at the wedding in Cana and was present during His crucifixion. Her life and actions proclaimed her faith and trust in God's plan, making her a powerful witness to God's work in the world.

Mary Magdalene: Mary Magdalene was the first to witness the risen Christ and was tasked with proclaiming this incredible news to the disciples. She became the first evangelist because she saw Jesus' resurrection. She boldly shared the news despite the potential disbelief and shock from others – she was too excited to care.

Mary, Jesus' mother and her namesake from Magdala, boldly shared their faith and experiences with others. Witnessing God's work and declaring your faith openly can inspire and encourage others to do the same.

Journaling Prompt

Reflect on a time in your life when you felt called to step out in faith like Mary, Jesus' mother, when she accepted God's plan for her life. How did you respond to that calling? What fears or uncertainties did you face? How did you overcome them? Consider Mary Magdalene's example, who demonstrated unwavering devotion and courage even in great challenges. How can you incorporate similar faithfulness and dedication into your daily life?

Chapter 8: Discovering Your God-Given Purpose

Have you ever heard the saying, "When the purpose of a thing is not known, abuse is inevitable"? This means you might misuse something if you don't know what it is intended for. For instance, say you have an awesome smartphone with fantastic camera quality, but you only use it to take blurry selfies. Why? You don't know all the neat tricks and features that come with the phone. You're missing out on the fun and incredible photos you could take because you don't understand the purpose of those little buttons and settings.

Imagine your smartphone is like a Swiss Army knife. You know, the one with the tiny tools that fold out—scissors, bottle openers, screwdrivers, the whole shebang. If you only ever use the knife, you're not getting the full potential. Right? The scissors would cut things, the bottle opener would open a soda, and the screwdriver would fix things around the house. Your new knife might have all these options, but that's not very efficient if you don't know all the tools for using the knife for everything.

Discovering your God-given purpose gives your life a deeper meaning.[23]

The same thing happens with humans. If you don't know your purpose, you might feel like that Swiss Army knife is only used to cut string. So, you only do things. You might not feel as happy or fulfilled because you don't do what you were truly meant to do. Learning what it is is like discovering that your smartphone camera has a slow-motion feature. Suddenly, life becomes a lot more exciting and meaningful.

This chapter will guide you through essential steps to help find and develop your God-given purpose. God-given, because everyone created and born comes for a reason or with a particular built-in skill set they only need to discover and harness. A section features biblical examples of characters discovering and fulfilling their God-given purpose.

If you struggle to find yours, this is your chance to look inward and uncover your unique, God-given purpose through this chapter's biblical teachings and examples.

If you're not in this category, that's fine. Read for a friend. If you don't have any friends, read anyway, you'll learn a thing or two.

The Concept of Divine Purpose and Its Significance in a Believer's Life

Like every strong and powerful building constructed according to the appropriate professional's architectural design, humans follow a blueprint to make the most of their lives. Every person is created for a unique reason, known as their divine purpose. This divine purpose is God's exclusive blueprint or plan for each individual.

This plan fits perfectly with who you are, your abilities, passions, and challenges because God is the architect. Like a piece in a puzzle has its perfect place, each person has a special role in God's big picture. However, it may take time to discover and understand this plan. The Lord says in Isaiah 55:8-9, *"For my thoughts are not your thoughts, neither are your ways my ways,"* declares the LORD. "As the heavens are higher than the earth, so are my ways higher than your ways and my thoughts than your thoughts.

God's purpose for your life is something He planned long before you were born. Jeremiah 1:5:

> *"Before I formed you in the womb I knew you, before you were born I set you apart; I appointed you as a prophet to the nations."*

He knows every detail about your life and has a reason for each step you take.

Understanding your divine purpose gives your life meaning and direction. When you discover what God wants you to do, you will feel peace and joy because you know you walk the path He has set for you. As rewarding and fulfilling as discovering your divine purpose can be, it is not always easy. It requires much patience and faith. Don't worry. The practical steps to discover and develop your God-given purpose are laid out in this chapter. First, here are a few biblical examples to learn from.

Biblical Figures Who Discovered and Fulfilled Their God-Given Purposes

The Bible has many stories of people who discovered their divine purpose and followed it with all their hearts. Finding and fulfilling your purpose is not always easy, but it is worth it. The following stories illustrate the significance of finding your God-given purpose:

Moses As a Leader

Moses is one of the most well-known figures in the Bible. He is known as the man whom God spoke to face to face. Exodus 33:11,

> *"The Lord would speak to Moses face to face, as one speaks to a friend. Then Moses would return to the camp, but his young aide Joshua son of Nun did not leave the tent."*

Imagine being Moses, growing up in a palace with all the riches and education you could desire. You are raised as an Egyptian prince, but you know you're different deep inside. Your people, the Israelites, do not live in palaces and don't have the same privileges as you.

One day, you see an Egyptian beating an Israelite man. In the heat of the moment, your passion flares up. You can't stand to see this injustice, so you step in and defend the Israelites, striking down the Egyptians. It might seem like a single act of anger, but it is a sign of the leader you are meant to become. God reveals your purpose, even if you don't fully understand it yet. You strongly desire to protect your people, stand up for them, and fight against their oppression.

However, you don't immediately become a respected leader – you had to flee from Egypt because of what you did. You end up in the desert, far from everything you ever knew. Yet, this is where God prepares you for greatness. Sometimes, you must go through hard times to understand what you are truly meant to do. In the quiet and stillness of the desert, God speaks to you. He shows you a burning bush, but the leaves stand tall like Shadrach, Meshach, and Abednego in the fiery furnace. God tells you to lead your people out of slavery. Finally, you know God's purpose for you—to be a deliverer.

So, you see, finding your purpose isn't always straightforward. Sometimes, it begins with a strong feeling or passion you care deeply about. You might not see the whole picture right away. For Moses, his anger over injustice became the first hint.

His God-given assignment wasn't a walk in the park. It was certainly not for the faint-hearted. Fortunately, Moses chose faith over fear and obeyed God. He returned to Egypt, confronted the Pharaoh, and performed miracles using God's power to show that God was real and powerful. God empowered Moses to lead the Israelites out of Egypt and across the Red Sea, where God performed a miracle by parting the waters so they could cross safely.

Moses led the people through the desert for 40 years, teaching them about God's laws and how to live as His people. Through it all, Moses fulfilled his divine purpose by trusting God and leading his people with courage and faith.

Esther, As a Queen

If someone had told Esther she would become queen of the Persian Empire while she and her people were exiled, she would probably suggest they nap to rest their heads.

Esther's story is a powerful example of how God can use anyone to fulfill a divine purpose, no matter how unlikely. Esther was the daughter of a Benjaminite, Abihail. Her parents died when she was young, so her uncle, Mordecai, took custody of her. By a miraculous twist of fate, the king of the Persian Empire removed his wife from the palace, and the search for a new wife began.

Esther wouldn't have believed she'd be the queen of the Persian Empire.[34]

Esther was chosen from among many young women. It seemed like a great honor, but it also put Esther in a difficult position. She had to hide her Jewish identity because to be a Jew in the king's palace was dangerous. That was risk number one.

Soon after Esther became queen, a wicked man named Haman, a high official in the king's court, became angry with Mordecai because Mordecai would not bow down to him. In his anger, Haman tricked the king into making a law to destroy all the Jews in the kingdom.

When Mordecai heard about this, he was highly upset and sent a message to Esther, asking her to go to the king and beg for their lives. Esther knew that going to the king without an invitation could mean death. However, Mordecai reminded her that she might be queen to save her people. Esther 4:14, *"For if you remain silent at this time, relief and deliverance for the Jews will arise from another place, but you and your father's family will perish. And who knows but that you have come to a royal position for such a time as this?"*

Esther had to be brave to take risk number two. She fasted and prayed for three days and asked the Jews to do the same. Esther 4:16, *"Go, gather together all the Jews who are in Susa, and fast for me. Do not eat or drink for three days, night or day. I and my maids will fast as you do. When this is done, I will go to the king, even though it is against the law. And if I perish, I perish."* She put on her royal robes and went to see the king. God gave her favor in the king's eyes, and he allowed her to speak. Esther invited the king and Haman to a banquet, and at the banquet, she revealed her Jewish identity and told the king about Haman's evil plan. The king was furious and ordered Haman to be punished. Ester's divine purpose saved the Jews.

Esther fulfilled her divine purpose by being courageous and trusting God. Her bravery saved her people and showed that God can use anyone to fulfill His plans, no matter how difficult the situation may seem.

Paul the Apostle

Paul, known as Saul, had a different story. Initially, he was not a follower of Jesus. He did not believe in Jesus, and those who followed Him were wrong.

Paul strictly followed the Jewish laws and believed the followers of Jesus broke those laws. He went as far as to hunt down Christians, imprisoning and torturing them. Acts 9:1-2, *"Meanwhile, Saul was still breathing out murderous threats against the Lord's disciples. He went to the high priest and asked him for letters to the synagogues in Damascus so that if he found any there who belonged to the Way, whether men or women, he might take them as prisoners to Jerusalem."* Paul thought he was doing the right thing. However, he fought against God's true purpose.

One day, Paul was on his way to Damascus to arrest more Christians, and something incredible happened. A bright light from heaven suddenly shone around him, and he fell to the ground. He heard a voice saying, *"Saul, Saul, why do you persecute me?"* Jesus spoke to him from heaven. Shocked and terrified, Paul asked, *"Who are you, Lord?"* Jesus replied, *"I am Jesus, whom you are persecuting"* (Acts 9:3-6). This encounter completely changed Paul's life. He realized Jesus was real and he had been wrong.

After this encounter, Paul became a follower of Jesus. He understood his purpose was to tell everyone about Jesus and the good news of salvation. Paul traveled to many places, preaching about Jesus, starting churches, and helping believers grow in their faith. His path came with immense challenges – he was imprisoned, beaten, faced many dangers, and even shipwrecked.

However, Paul knew he was doing God's will and continued with vigor. He wrote many letters to the Churches, now part of the Bible. He used the letters to teach and encourage Christians to continue their faith.

Apostle Paul dedicated his life to sharing the gospel of Jesus Christ and God's love and excelled because this was his divine purpose.

Understanding Your Divine Purpose

Like Moses, Esther, and Paul, every believer has a divine purpose, a unique role God planned for them to fulfill. Discovering this purpose is not easy and usually takes time. Sometimes, you must go through difficult situations to grow and learn more about yourself and God's plan for you. These challenges help shape and prepare you for God's tasks. God's purpose for everyone is always good. Jeremiah 29:11, *"For I know the plans I have for you," declares the LORD, "plans to prosper you and not to harm you, plans to give you hope and a future."*

You must stay close to God to find your divine purpose. God gives you hope and a future. Spending time in prayer, reading the Bible, and talking to other believers who can provide you with sound advice and support will guide you to your divine purpose. Pay attention to what you are naturally drawn to and what you enjoy doing and are good at. Sometimes, God speaks to you through your desires and talents to guide you toward living a life full of joy and fulfillment to help others.

You can't discover your divine purpose and then relax. You must catch and run with the vision, or you will be like the man who keeps the talent hidden. Matthew 25:24-28:

"Then the man who had received one bag of gold came. 'Master,' he said, 'I knew that you are a hard man, harvesting where you have not sown and gathering where you have not scattered seed. So, I was afraid and went out and hid your gold in the ground. See, here is what belongs to you.' His master replied, 'You wicked, lazy servant! So, you knew that I harvest where I have not sown and gather where I have not scattered seed? Well then, you should have put my money on deposit with the bankers, so that when I returned I would have received it back with interest." So, take the bag of gold from him and give it to the one who

has ten bags. For whoever has will be given more, and they will have an abundance. Whoever does not have, even what they have will be taken from them."

You can see how dangerous it is to find your purpose and sit on it. Once you find your purpose, don't let anyone tell you otherwise. Follow it with all your heart, like Moses, Esther, and Paul did. Everyone has their unique path. Sometimes, finding and following God's purpose might require leaving close friends or loved ones, but you must be ready to do so. It could mean joining forces with people you never imagined speaking to, but you're not the one in charge. God is. 1 Thessalonians 5:24, "The one who calls you is faithful, and he will do it."

You might face challenges and difficulties, but you can trust that God is with you, helping you and giving you strength. He promised to never leave nor forsake you. He will help you fulfill your destiny.

Practical Steps for Identifying and Developing Your God-Given Purpose

Finding your God-given purpose is a big deal. But don't worry. This section breaks it down into small, easy, practical steps. In the quest to find your purpose, you must look at the clues: your strengths, passions, and experiences. Guess what? God plants tiny hints around you from the time you're born to help you figure it out. Here's where to look for:

God plants tiny seeds in your life that reveal your life purpose.[25]

Look at the Things You Naturally Excel In

The first place to check is what you're naturally good at—your strengths. These are things that come easily to you, maybe things you don't notice because they feel like second nature. Do your friends compare you to a famous singer because of how well you sing at home? Can you whip up a delicious meal without breaking a sweat (and without burning the kitchen down—bonus points for that)? Perhaps you have an excellent memory and reproduce an image you see on paper with intricate details, or maybe you are the best at organizing things. These are hints as to your true purpose.

You might think, "But I'm not good at anything." Here's a secret you should know for free: everyone has something they excel in, including you. It might be something small, like always being on time (not everyone has that gift) or a talent for making people laugh. Think about what people compliment you on or what comes naturally to you. Write them down. You could be on to something with those clues.

What Are You Passionate About?

For Moses, he was ready to fight for his people. For Paul, he was ready to die for what he believed in. Now, ask yourself, what is one thing that sets your heart on fire? What could you talk about for hours without getting bored? What makes you come alive? When God calls you, He often starts with something that already stirs your heart. Your passion is not random. It's a clue to what you are meant to do. Like Moses, you might go through a desert period of waiting and preparation. Time doesn't necessarily mean delay. It is God shaping and preparing you for your purpose. Your passions are another signpost pointing you toward your God-given purpose.

Consult Your Yesterdays

This is something not everyone does. Most people are all about the present and moving toward the future, living like yesterday never existed. However, in the quest to find your purpose, you must visit your past. So, try something in this 'now moment.' Look back at your life. Sometimes, thinking about the past is not fun, especially if it is mostly unpleasant. However, your experiences shape you.

Everything that happened then was no accident. God uses everything. Think about the good, the bad, and the funny (like when you tried to dye your hair and ended up with a color not found in nature). What did you learn from the experiences? How have they made you stronger, wiser, or more compassionate? Write these down because they will guide you toward your purpose.

Step Out, Try Something New and Explore

This is where it gets exciting. Once you've done some soul-searching, it's time to act. The wisest man in the Bible said in Proverbs 14:23, *"All hard work brings a profit, but mere talk leads only to poverty."* It's not enough to wonder about your purpose and keep talking about it. Start trying new things! Your purpose may be something you haven't tried yet. Maybe you admire people who do it. Explore while you still have the time. If you think you might be called to help others, volunteer somewhere. If you feel a pull toward creativity, start painting or writing. Don't be afraid to step out of your comfort zone. Your God-given purpose won't pay you a surprise visit if all you do is sit on the couch and watch TV all day. Come out of your cocoon.

Pray and Ask God for Guidance

This is the most important step. Miss this one, and you might miss your way. The Bible records in Proverbs 14:12, *"There is a way that appears to be right but in the end, it leads to death."* God must be involved. As a human, your knowledge and power are limited. The good news is that you don't have to figure it out by yourself. Isn't that a relief? God will guide you. He knows your purpose. So, use quiet time to pray and ask Him to show you the way.

When you pray, be honest with God. Tell Him about your worries, hopes, and confusions. The answer could come in several ways: feeling peaceful, a new idea, or a conversation with a friend. Keep your heart open and trust that God is leading you where you need to go.

Prayer is crucial to discovering your God-given purpose. You must pray frequently, ask God for guidance, and listen carefully to His voice during your purpose-discovering journey. It can happen through reading the Bible, talking with other believers, or paying attention to what you feel passionate about. God often speaks quietly through your thoughts, feelings, and people around you. There will be more about prayer in the next and final chapter.

As you grow in your relationship with Him, He will reveal more of His plan for you. When you finally understand your purpose, it changes everything about how you live. You're expected to make choices in line with God's plan, giving you peace knowing you're doing what you were born for.

Journaling Prompt

Create a purpose vision board in your journal. Gather images, quotes, and Bible verses that resonate with your understanding of your God-given purpose. Arrange them on a board to create a visual representation of your calling. Use this board as a daily reminder to stay focused on your divine purpose.

Chapter 9: Developing a Consistent Prayer Life

Many believers make the mistake of only praying to God when in need or afraid. Remembering to pray when facing a problem too big to handle or when scared and unsure is easy. In times like this, you quickly pour your heart out, telling Him about your troubles, fears, and worries because you desperately seek His intervention.

While it's good to pray in these times because God wants you to bring your needs and fears to Him, prayer is much more than a tool for emergencies or solving your problems. Prayer is a way to build a deep and personal relationship with God.

Praying consistently enriches your relationship with God.[26]

Imagine if you only talked to a close friend when you needed something or were afraid. The relationship would feel shallow and one-sided, wouldn't it? The same is true with God. He desires a relationship with you based on more than your needs. God wants you to come to Him in all situations. 1 Peter 5:7, *"Cast all your anxiety on him because he cares for you."* It doesn't matter if you're happy, sad, joyful, or grieving. He wants to always fellowship with you.

Making time to pray and study the bible regularly is telling the Lord you value your relationship with Him. Tell him everything. He will listen and help you. Developing a consistent prayer life tells God you want to know Him more deeply, not because of what He can do for you, but because of who He is. God knows you're using Him only for the one-issue-to-worry-about prayer. Instead, consciously seek Him daily, spend time in His presence, and talk to Him about everything. You will build a rich and lasting relationship with your Heavenly Father, brick by brick.

This chapter will help you develop a consistent prayer life because you'll need it while searching for and developing your God-given purpose.

Benefits of Regular Pray and Bible Study

Increase in Faith Level

Praying and reading the Bible daily helps your faith grow stronger, like exercising makes your body stronger. The more you learn about God's love and promises, the more you trust Him. You saw how God helped people in the Bible. Start believing He can help you, too. Whenever you pray, you're showing trust in God and building faith over time. Romans 10:17, *"So then faith comes by hearing, and hearing by the word of God."* Hebrews 11:6, *"And without faith, it is impossible to please God, because anyone who comes to Him must believe that He exists and that He rewards those who earnestly seek Him."*

Increase in Peace

Regular prayer and Bible study bring peace into your life. When you pray, you give your worries and problems to God, like handing over a heavy bag to someone to carry it. Reading the Bible reminds you of God's promises and care for you, helping you feel calmer and less stressed. You feel peace, knowing God is always with you. Philippians 4:6-7:

"Do not be anxious about anything, but in every situation, by prayer and petition, with thanksgiving, present your requests to God. And the peace of God, which transcends all understanding, will guard your hearts and your minds in Christ Jesus."

Isaiah 26:3:

"You will keep in perfect peace those whose minds are steadfast because they trust in you."

Increase in Guidance

If you cultivate the habit of praying (asking God) for guidance, you will see how real God is in your life. Jeremiah 33:3 says, *"Call to me and I will answer you and tell you great and unsearchable things you do not know."* You ask for guidance because you do not know. God can show you the right path, the best decisions, and the people who will help you grow. Regular Bible study enables you to understand God's guidance better. Psalm 119:105, *"Your word is a lamp for my feet, a light on my path."* When you read the Bible often, you learn about what God wants for your life. You start to feel more confident in knowing what to do.

Biblical Examples of People with a Disciplined Prayer Life

Daniel

Daniel was a man in the Old Testament with a disciplined prayer life. The Bible states that Daniel prayed to God three times daily, kneeling by his window facing Jerusalem (Daniel 6:10). It was a habit he would not break even if his life depended on it. He continued to pray even when the king made a law that anyone who prayed to anyone other than the king would be thrown into a den of lions. But he wasn't afraid. Like he said in Daniel 11:32, *"...but the people who know their God shall stand firm and take action."* (ESV)

Jesus

Jesus is the perfect role model of a disciplined prayer life. Even though He had a very busy life, He made time to pray for an hour or more. Jesus traveled about teaching people, healing the sick, and performing miracles, yet He prayed regularly. He often went to quiet places early in the morning or late at night to pray to His Father in heaven. Mark 1:35:

"Very early in the morning, while it was still dark, Jesus got up, left the house, and went off to a solitary place, where he prayed."

Matthew 14:23:

"After he had dismissed them, he went up on a mountainside by himself to pray. Later that night, he was there alone."

Luke 6:12:

"One of those days Jesus went out to a mountainside to pray, and spent the night praying to God."

The Early Christians

The early Christians were the multitude who followed Jesus wherever He went. So, when He ascended to heaven, they would come together as a group, often meeting in each other's homes to share meals and pray. The Bible says they were *"Devoted to the apostles' teaching and to fellowship, to the breaking of bread and to prayer"* (Acts 2:42). They were very committed to spending time together, learning more about God, and praying. In Acts 12:5-7, they prayed fervently, and an angel rescued Peter.

Practical Tips for Creating a Prayer Schedule

Setting Specific Times for Prayer

When will you most likely have a few quiet minutes throughout your day? Is it early in the morning before the house wakes up or in the evening after the kids are in bed? Find a time that works best for you, and try to stick to it every day. Setting a regular time helps make prayer a habit. You might start with praying in the morning when you wake up or praying at night as the last thing you do before bed. Or it could be both.

Setting Specific Places for Prayer

Just as having a specific time is important, it can also help to have a special place for prayer. This should be somewhere you feel comfortable and can focus on talking to God. It could be a corner of your bedroom, a cozy chair in your living room, or a spot in your garden. The aim is to ensure you don't get distracted. It helps you feel closer to God because it's just you and Him in that moment.

Methods of Prayer

Prayer of Adoration

A prayer of adoration is when you praise God for who He is. In this prayer, you tell Him how wonderful, powerful, and loving He is. An example of this prayer is in Psalm 104:1-4:

"Praise the Lord, my soul. Lord my God, you are very great; you are clothed with splendor and majesty. The Lord wraps himself in light as with a garment; he stretches out the heavens like a tent and lays the beams of his upper chambers on their waters..."

Prayer of Confession

1 John 1:8:

"If we claim to be without sin, we deceive ourselves and the truth is not in us."

This is a prayer where you humbly tell God what you've done wrong and ask for His forgiveness. Being honest with God about your mistakes is crucial. 1 John 1:9 says:

"If we confess our sins, he is faithful and just and will forgive us our sins and purify us from all unrighteousness."

God is always ready to forgive you when you come to Him with a genuinely repentant heart.

Prayer of confession.[27]

Prayer of Thanksgiving

In this prayer, thank God for all the good things in your life. Don't focus on what you don't have. Instead, count your blessings and name them one by one, like the Psalmist says. You will see you have more than enough reasons to give thanks to God. 1 Chronicles 16:34, *"Give thanks to the Lord, for he is good; his love endures forever."*

Prayer of Supplication

This is the prayer where you ask for God's help with your needs and the needs of others. You can bring it to God, whether it's something big or small. The Bible says in Ephesians 3:20 that God *"...is able to do immeasurably more than all we ask or imagine, according to his power that is at work within us..."* So, ask him for help.

Suggestions for Integrating Bible Study into Daily Routines

A devotional is a short reading, usually including a Bible verse and a short reflection or story to help you contemplate God's Word. You can read this in the morning with your prayer or any time during the day. It may be brief, but it can set a positive tone for your day and remind you of God's presence.

You can follow a Bible reading plan to guide you on which verses to read each day. Many plans are available online. Some are designed to be read in a year. Others focus on specific topics or books of the Bible. Choose a plan that interests you and fits into your schedule. You can combine your prayer time with Bible study. As you go to God in prayer and Bible study, you will *"... hear a voice behind you, saying, "This is the way; walk in it."* (Isaiah 30:21).

Journaling Prompt

Create a weekly prayer and Bible study schedule. Plan out specific times each day dedicated to prayer and reading the Bible. Use your journal to track your progress, noting insights or answered prayers. Reflect on how this routine strengthens your relationship with God.

Conclusion

As a woman, your life assumes many roles and responsibilities. You may be a mother, a daughter, a sister, a wife, or a friend. Between juggling work, caring for your family, and managing a home, you're usually left feeling overwhelmed. Hence, you need to schedule time for Bible study and prayer. These spiritual tools will help you find peace, guidance, and strength to carry out your daily activities efficiently.

Congratulations on finishing this spiritual journey with this guide. You have invested time and resources in your life and will surely reap the benefits. You discovered how God helped women in the past. You learned about women like Esther, the courageous orphan turned Queen, and Ruth, who was loyal and kind. All the Bible characters featured in this book had moral lessons you could learn from.

Studying the Bible teaches you much about God's love and His will. Studying the Bible and becoming more consistent in prayer connects you with God personally, and you feel His presence enveloping you like a warm blanket. Pray regularly turns you into the lady with a laid-back vibe. You feel and look calmer and less stressed because you know God is listening and everything is working in your favor. The Bible says in Romans 8:28, "And we know that in all things God works for the good of those who love him, who have been called according to his purpose."

Combining Bible study and prayer helps you better decide because when you ask God for guidance, you are confident He will show you the right path. Bible study and prayer help you build stronger relationships. You learn to love and forgive others from Jesus' teaching about God's love and forgiveness. You become more patient and kinder, improving your relationships with your family, friends, and others. You learn to be more understanding and compassionate, seeing others as God sees them.

Finding your divine purpose and direction in life has never been easier. As a woman, you may wonder about your purpose or what you should do with your life. The Bible teaches that God has a plan for everyone, including you. Here's some more good news: You have a guide to refer to whenever you feel lost or confused.

Bible study and consistent prayer are not things you should do. It is something you must do if you wish to excel in all areas of life and fulfill your divine purpose on Earth. Walk with God and watch Him shape you into the glorious queen He created you to be. It is your time to manifest.

Before you close this book, say a prayer with these Bible verses:

- **Psalm 25:4-5:** *"Show me your ways, Lord, teach me your paths. Guide me in your truth and teach me, for you are God my Savior, and my hope is in you all day long."*
- **Psalm 119:35:** *"Direct me in the path of your commands, for there I find delight."*
- **Psalm 86:11:** *"Teach me your way, Lord, that I may rely on your faithfulness; give me an undivided heart, that I may fear your name."*
- **Psalm 19:14:** *"May these words of my mouth and this meditation of my heart be pleasing in your sight, Lord, my Rock, and my Redeemer."*

If you enjoyed this book, a review on Amazon would be greatly appreciated because it would mean a lot to hear from you.

To leave a review:
1. Open your camera app.
2. Point your mobile device at the QR code.
3. The review page will appear in your web browser.

Thanks for your support!

Check out another book in the series

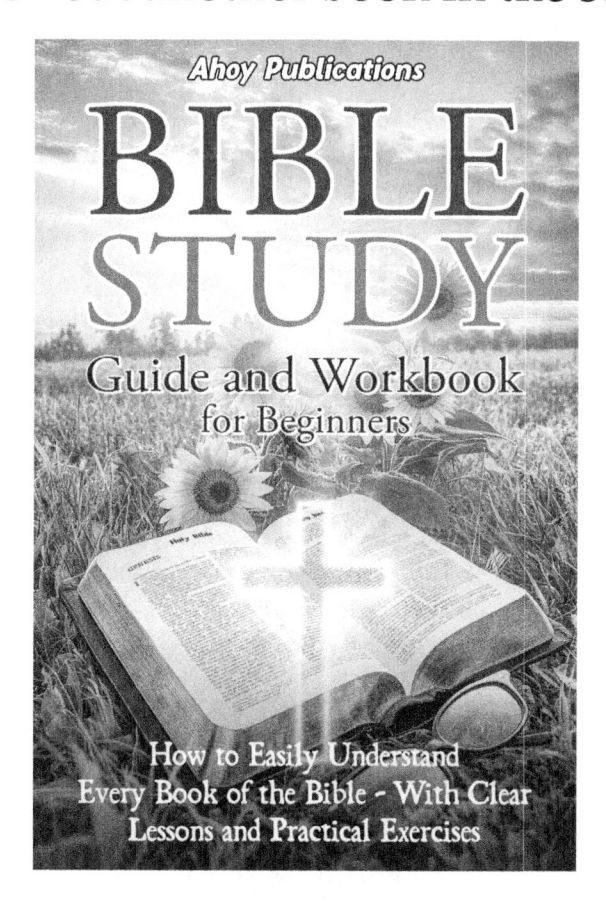

Ahoy Publications

BIBLE STUDY

Guide and Workbook
for Beginners

How to Easily Understand
Every Book of the Bible - With Clear
Lessons and Practical Exercises

Welcome Aboard, Check Out This Limited-Time Free Bonus!

Ahoy, reader! Welcome to the Ahoy Publications family, and thanks for snagging a copy of this book! Since you've chosen to join us on this journey, we'd like to offer you something special.

Check out the link below for a FREE e-book filled with delightful facts about American History.

But that's not all - you'll also have access to our exclusive email list with even more free e-books and insider knowledge. Well, what are ye waiting for? Click the link below to join and set sail toward exciting adventures in American History.

Access your bonus here
https://ahoypublications.com/
Or, Scan the QR code!

References

10 Best Psalms About Trusting God (And Not the World). (2020, November 15). Psalm 91. https://psalm91.com/2020/11/15/10-best-psalms-about-trusting-god-and-not-the-world/

10 Psalms of Trust in God's Goodness and Care for His People – BibleTruths. (2017, November 22). BibleTruths. https://www.bibletruths.org/10-psalms-trust-god-goodness-care/

Anderson, E. (2024, July 12). 5 Themes From the Psalms – The Rebelution. The Rebelution. https://www.therebelution.com/blog/2024/07/5-themes-from-the-psalms/

Brodie, J. (2020, October 26). 6 Beautiful Psalms for Encouragement for You in Your Daily Life. Christianity.com; Salem Web Network. https://www.christianity.com/wiki/bible/psalms-to-encourage-you-in-your-daily-life.html

Bucher, M. (2018, November 3). Who Was Mary Magdalene in the Bible? – 5 Questions Answered. Bible Study Tools; Salem Web Network. https://www.biblestudytools.com/bible-study/topical-studies/who-was-mary-magdalene.html

Carroll, J. (2006, June). Who Was Mary Magdalene? Smithsonian; Smithsonian.com. https://www.smithsonianmag.com/history/who-was-mary-magdalene-119565482/

Fr. Stavros Akrotirianakis. (2020, April 28). Psalm 11—Trusting in God Must Be a Consistent Theme. Orthodox Christian Network. https://myocn.net/psalm-11-trusting-in-god-must-be-a-consistent-theme/

Guiley, R. E. (2021, December 7). The Importance of Prayer and Meditation. Unity.org. https://www.unity.org/article/importance-prayer-and-meditation

Lucey, C. (2020, December 29). Who Was Mary the Mother of Jesus? Christianity.com. https://www.christianity.com/wiki/holidays/who-was-mary-the-mother-of-jesus.html

The Role of Psalms in Christian Worship. (2024, June 5). Digital Bible; Digital Bible. https://digitalbible.ca/article-page/modern-topics-what-does-the-bible-say-about-psalm

WHN. (2010, December 26). Mary, Mother of Jesus Christ. Women's History Network. https://womenshistorynetwork.org/mary-mother-of-jesus-christ/

Worshiping with the Psalms. (2015). Reformed Worship. https://www.reformedworship.org/article/june-2016/worshiping-psalms

Image Sources

[1] https://www.pexels.com/photo/person-holding-brown-holy-bible-5199796/
[2] designed by Freepik. https://www.freepik.com/free-photo/words-smart-goals-with-dart-target-dartboard_1131515.htm
[3] https://www.pexels.com/photo/close-up-shot-of-a-person-reading-a-bible-5206052/
[4] https://www.pexels.com/photo/close-up-photo-of-bible-4654082/
[5] https://www.pexels.com/photo/silhouette-of-man-with-angel-wings-during-dawn-2043837/
[6] designed by Freepik. https://www.freepik.com/free-vector/gradient-ascension-day-illustration_25001742.htm
[7] https://www.pexels.com/photo/rosary-on-holy-bible-5875398/
[8] https://www.pexels.com/photo/close-up-of-the-bible-5124915/
[9] designed by Freepik. https://www.freepik.com/free-vector/hand-drawn-moses-illustration_37370323.htm
[10] designed by Freepik. https://www.freepik.com/free-photo/front-view-person-making-heart-from-holy-book-pages_9469595.htm
[11] designed by Freepik. https://www.freepik.com/free-photo/vertical-shot-female-wearing-biblical-robe-with-her-hands-up-towards-sky-praying_8981177.htm
[12] designed by Freepik. https://www.freepik.com/free-photo/portrait-queen-with-royal-crown_40391193.htm
[13] https://www.pexels.com/photo/writing-typography-blur-bokeh-11506026/
[14] https://www.pexels.com/photo/a-man-in-brown-robe-holding-a-shepherd-s-crook-7360551/
[15] https://www.pexels.com/photo/waterfall-in-mountainous-terrain-with-steep-slopes-5668668/
[16] https://www.pexels.com/photo/open-bible-book-lying-on-white-blanket-among-decorations-22711043/

[17] https://www.pexels.com/photo/silhouette-image-of-person-praying-1615776/

[18] https://www.pexels.com/photo/sheep-grazing-on-dramatic-cliff-edge-28544171/

[19] designed by Freepik. https://www.freepik.com/free-photo/person-wearing-biblical-robe-standing-water-with-blurred_14256138.htm

[20] https://www.pexels.com/photo/new-testament-book-5421124/

[21] designed by Freepik. https://www.freepik.com/free-photo/shallow-focus-shot-jesus-christ-giving-piece-bread-female-wearing-biblical-robe_13291250.htm

[22] https://www.pexels.com/photo/mother-mary-and-christ-figurine-on-black-background-51524/

[23] https://www.pexels.com/photo/colorful-cutouts-of-the-word-purpose-4116640/

[24] https://www.pexels.com/photo/ancient-wall-decoration-5624531/

[25] https://www.pexels.com/photo/shallow-focus-of-sprout-401213/

[26] https://www.pexels.com/photo/woman-wearing-white-long-sleeved-shirt-praying-3285947/

[27] designed by Freepik. https://www.freepik.com/free-photo/close-up-priest-talking-with-person_22814903.htm

Printed in Great Britain
by Amazon